THE NEW
RATIONAL
MANAGER

Charles H. **KEPNER**
Benjamin B. **TREGOE**

For information address Princeton Research Press
P.O. Box 704, Research Road, Princeton, New Jersey 08540

Library of Congress Catalog Card No.: 80-84367
Tregoe, Benjamin B. and Charles H. Kepner
The New Rational Manager.
Princeton, N.J.: Kepner-Tregoe, Inc.
224 p.
8101   801017

Book and jacket design: Pam Forde Graphics

CONTENTS

ACKNOWLEDGMENT

A great many people have contributed to the writing of this book, far too many to name. Thousands of individuals have used the procedures and concepts of Rational Management on the job, against real concerns and problems, and have then told us of their experiences. More than a thousand client organizations around the world have shared information with us, often of a highly proprietary nature, in an effort to learn more about Rational Process. Several thousand Program Leaders have also shared their insights with us. Our own colleagues and associates have been particularly helpful. We could not have written this book without them, for it largely reports the experiences of others in using and promoting these ideas. We wish to thank all of these people for the contributions they have made. They are the true authors of this book.

We wish also to acknowledge the assistance of The Hudson Group, Inc., Pleasantville, New York, in the preparation of this book.

INTRODUCTION

In 1957 we were doing social science research with the RAND Corporation. In the course of our work, we witnessed a number of decisions in government agencies and in private industry that ranged in quality from questionable to catastrophic. Wondering how such poor decisions ever came to be made, we decided to look into their histories. We found that most of these decisions were bad because certain important pieces of available information had been ignored, discounted, or given insufficient attention. We concluded that the *process* of gathering and organizing information for decision making needed improvement. A more *rational approach*—one devised to collect and make the best use of all important pieces of information—would be a vast improvement over the countless disorderly approaches we had observed.

RAND was not interested in our pursuing this line of inquiry, so we left the organization and set up our own company. Kepner-Tregoe and Associates consisted of two people with a few half-formed ideas and a pint-sized office in a garage. We studied the literature on decision making, or "problem solving" as it was termed in those days, and found little that was helpful. We then went into the field to talk with and observe real managers at work—and we began to learn.

We found that "problem solving" was not a very useful term: There was no single mental process a manager could adopt to focus on all situations that might arise. In practice, the most effective managers we observed used variations of four distinct routines or patterns of thinking, in handling problems and decisions. In time we would refine and consolidate these routines into four rational processes for managing.

The first basic routine concerned organizational skills.

The best managers—that is, those considered by other managers as most effective and successful—approached the job of managing in an orderly way. They asked pertinent questions, quickly recognizing and isolating situations of current or potential importance for closer scrutiny. They set priorities quickly and accurately. They knew when and how to delegate authority while retaining an appropriate degree of control.

The less effective managers we observed did not have these organizational skills. They tended to name and rank priorities according to the crisis of the moment or to their superiors' most recent directives. They were not sure of when to delegate activities or what degree of control to maintain once they had done so. Their lack of control was sometimes justified as "flexibility" and often defended as the antithesis of "rigidity."

Even at this early point in our observations, we saw a definite correlation between the level of a manager's organizational skills (including those needed to handle everyday details) and his or her accomplishment in the more visible activities of problem solving and decision making. The success of the play, more often than not, was dependent upon the setting of the stage.

The most effective managers were also the best investigators—a characteristic of their second basic routine. From the announcement of a problem until its resolution, they appeared to follow a clear formula in both the orderly sequence and the quality of their questions and actions. In fact, when something went wrong, without a ready explanation, these managers asked remarkably similar questions to determine whether available information was relevant or irrelevant, important or trivial, critical or marginally useful. Since the same information, in the hands of different but equally experienced and intelligent managers, might result in distinctly different results, it was evident that successful problem solving involved more than the availability of information. *Equally critical was the quality of logic applied to that information.*

A third basic routine concerned decision making—a process requiring a pattern of thinking totally unlike that used in problem solving. On the one hand a problem exists when something has gone wrong. To solve it we must understand why it has gone wrong. Only then can we take appropriate action. A decision is required, however, when we are faced with alternative courses of action. To make a good choice, we must understand all the factors that must be satisfied. In our field study, once we made this clear distinction between the two processes, we recognized why "problem solving" —describing "what the manager does"—had been such a misleading, catch-all term: It did not distinguish between problem solving and the very different process of decision making.

If the two processes had anything in common, it was that the more effective managers tended to ask the same kinds of questions in approaching and making decisions. They may have expressed themselves in individual ways, but the similarities were remarkable. Had they discovered these sequences because they were more capable managers? Or was their effectiveness a consequence of a natural tendency to think and act in these sequences? Whatever the answer may be, the result was an optimal sequence of questions and activities that led to better-than-average problem solving and decision making.

A fourth routine we observed protected the product of the manager's actions. Once a problem had been solved or once a decision had been made, the effective manager went the extra mile to ensure that the problem would stay at bay, that the decision would remain successful. Precise techniques varied from one individual to another, but similarities in approach outnumbered differences. There was a clear-cut best way of troubleshooting the future, and it could be described step by step.

From our observations, we refined the best techniques and routines used by these successful managers into a body of four rational processes for effective management, and we began to teach what we had learned. We taught managers how to gather and use information for problem solving and decision making. To create learning vehicles, we used fictionalized accounts of actual events, problems, and decisions. For good reason the resulting cases had the ring of truth.

We invented the Apex Company, which was beset by perplexities, irritations, and disasters borrowed from companies we had visited. The first group of managers we trained worked through these cases, just as managers do in our programs today. They began by applying their own approaches for understanding, resolving, or reaching a recommendation about each test situation. Then the ideas of rational process were introduced, and the managers restudied the cases to determine how nearly their own techniques resembled Kepner-Tregoe techniques—the embodiment of thousands of hours of observing *what worked best for successful managers*. How did their own investigative techniques compare with these? Their approaches to decision making? Their methods for setting priorities? The comparisons went on to include all of the major, critical functions of managing.

Using our techniques, the managers we trained improved their use of information, enabling them to move directly to the resolution of their own problems and decisions. Groups of managers, similarly instructed, worked together more efficiently than ever because they had been given a common language and common approaches to use on shared tasks. The resultant savings could be measured and documented.

By this time we had a name for our program: we called it *rational management*. Today the vast majority of people who learn to use rational process are trained within their own organizations by line managers who have been prepared by Kepner-Tregoe. These Program Leaders introduce and maintain the ideas and methods we have described. They often function in addition as internal consultants to their own organizations, lending their expertise with rational processes.

The programs they teach have not changed much over the years *because the elements of problem solving and decision making do not change*. Only the situations change—the contents upon which a rational process is focused. Since it is the *how* that concerns us, not the *what* and *why* of a situation, any necessary modifications and alterations involve only the expansion of basic principles of the processes themselves. Despite increasing complexity and proliferation of information, the stability of the process continues to create its obvious benefits.

Commanding systematic techniques and specific lines of inquiry and activity, the effective manager is secure in knowing that all necessary questions are being asked, all critical information considered, and all bases covered. This consistency of approach means that one manager can study another's Kepner-Tregoe analysis at any point in its formulation and pick up its thread immediately.

From this condition of security comes the freedom for the manager to work imaginatively and creatively in pursuit of the resolution, choice, or plan that is not only safe and correct, but perhaps unusual or outstanding as well.

● ● ●

Finally, a word about the objectives of this book. Our intention is to make the clearest possible statement about how and why the rational processes work, to make suggestions for maximizing their effectiveness, and to show what our clients have achieved through their original and imaginative uses of the processes. At the same time we will explain the conditions needed to support the kinds of organization-wide programs that have grown so tremendously since we wrote *The Rational Manager* in 1965.

In keeping with the dictum that has well served both our clients and Kepner-Tregoe, all examples that appear in this book reflect the true experiences of active managers at work in real organizations.

CHAPTER 1

The Premises of Rational Management

Introduction:
The Search for Organizational Effectiveness

The organization is one of mankind's all-time great inventions. An organization is intended to operate as one unit, with all its parts in efficient coordination. But too often it does not. The parts operate at disparate levels of efficiency, or they overlap, or they work against one another's best interests—therefore against the best interests of the organization as a whole. There is misunderstanding and miscommunication, sometimes by accident and sometimes not. Things get done, progress is made. But not enough of the right things get done as well as they should. Progress, however it is defined, does not meet expectations.

The search has been on for many years to find ways of improving organizational effectiveness. Everyone agrees that there is room for improvement, that the organization as we know it is not perfect. Failure of the organization to perform as a functional unit limits full realization of its potential. What to do about it and how to improve the organization to make it more productive and efficient are subjects of great disagreement.

In 1965 we wrote *The Rational Manager*. In that book we described the concepts and techniques we had developed for using information in problem solving, decision making, and planning for the future. During the period before and after 1965, we conducted week-long workshops for twenty or so executives at a time, offering intensive training in the use of these concepts and techniques. How the executives would apply what they had learned when they returned to their jobs was left largely up to them. Nearly everyone left the workshop determined to put the new ideas to work.

Not surprisingly, results were better in the organizations that promoted and encouraged the continuing use of these ideas. Where there was little or no encouragement to use the ideas, where there were few or no other people who also had been exposed to them, their use dwindled.

Organizations recognized these facts. "Show us how to use these ideas on a team basis" became a familiar refrain. Since the mid-1960s, we have learned a great deal about the ways in which our concepts and techniques can be used on a shared basis by the members of an organization in a common approach to addressing the tasks of problem solving, decision making, and planning. We have learned how to help our clients establish the teamwork they have come to value at least as highly as discrete management skills. From these clients we have learned what works and what does not. This book, then, has grown out of the fifteen years of experience we and they have amassed since the writing of *The Rational Manager*—fifteen years of research, trial, error, and innovation based on what they have told us they want and need.

The Group and the Team

When interacting in a common cause, people can become a cohesive group. Understanding one another as individuals, being consciously sensitive to one another, and knowing how to adapt to individual peculiarities are what make a functioning group that will hold together. Common regard and the psychological benefits that group members derive from the association make group activity desirable and reasonable to achieve. Such a group, however, is not a team.

A team is built primarily on the technical capabilities of its members working in pursuit of specific goals, only secondarily on attraction among the members as individuals. The members of a team must be able to tolerate one another enough to work closely together. Beyond this, all the members must be committed to a common goal and the same set of procedures for achieving that goal.

An athletic team does not win a game because the members like to be together. It wins because it plays smart, knows how to play the game better than the opposition, avoids unnecessary errors, and pulls together as a coordinated unit. Camaraderie may grow out of mutual respect for one another's abilities, but this is usually the result, not the purpose, of the team. Most certainly it is not the mechanism that makes the team succeed. The overall goal of a team is to win, and every member keeps this firmly in mind. But when you analyze *how* a game is won, you discover that it happens because all the players know what to do and how to coordinate their efforts.

Building a Management Team

Consider now the successful management team, so fervently sought after. The members are specialists in all required areas of expertise, with unique contributions to make by virtue of unique experiences and knowledge. They are necessarily different sorts of people: Here is the entrepreneur with an aggressive, driving nature and quick insights; the financial expert, with a measuring kind of intelligence and a finely developed ability to move patiently while being pushed; the sales and marketing executive, with unbounded enthusiasm and, sometimes, unbounded impatience; the director of research and development, able to control the balance between the feasible and the desirable; and the production manager, motivated chiefly by the realities of what it takes each day to get the product out the back door. All these men and women were hired because they were different and had different things to offer. They might not choose each other's company for a weekend trip, but given common organizational goals to work toward and a method for coordinating their efforts, they can become an unbeatable management team.

What kind of method for coordinating their efforts? One consisting of simple, common, sensible guidelines and procedures expressed in a commonly understood language: guidelines and procedures that bridge the differences within the team and its individual functions, guidelines and procedures the team can use jointly to carry out responsibilities without inhibiting individual contributions or adding new, unessential tasks.

Just as you must give the members of an athletic team routines and techniques that will coordinate their individual abilities in order to win the game, you must give a management team common guidelines and procedures for gathering, sharing, and using information to solve problems, make decisions, and safeguard the organization's future. Now extend the analogy a bit further. Sports rise above local language and culture. A Brazilian soccer player can play the game in any country. He can move from one team to another because the rules are international and transcultural. The skills of good team-playing are transferable in sports, and so it is in management. A competent manager can be a member of many teams, contributing wherever there is a need for his or her skills and experience, an active partner in the coordinated activity that makes an organization go.

One of our clients, a large commodity-trading corporation with operations in twenty countries, faced a series of difficult decisions. Should the company continue to rent storage and handling facilities in the Port of Antwerp or move to some other location in Europe? If the company were to seek another location, where? Once a location had been agreed upon, how should the company operate it? Build new facilities? Rent existing ones? Form a joint venture with someone having such facilities? Once the type of operation was decided, what would be the best way to communicate and sell the recommendation to all the others involved? How would foreign exchange, time and cost of shipping, and sales and marketing considerations be integrated into this decision?

A task force of executives from five nations convened in Europe. They were from different organizational levels, with different kinds of expertise and different native tongues. Many of them had never worked together—some had never even met—but all of them were familiar with Kepner-Tregoe decision-making concepts. Although some of the managers had originally learned the concepts in French, German, or Italian, everyone was fluent enough in English to use that as the common language.

Over the next two days they worked their way through the entire set of decisions. "They knew where to start, what questions to ask, what to do," said the Vice President for International Operations. "They really did work as a team. With that approach to decision making, a term such as 'objectives' had only one, very specific meaning. Such a simple thing, you might think, but it meant that with a minimum of internal translation, each person was able to grasp what was going on all along the way, to ask and answer questions so that everybody understood what everybody else was saying. Which is not usual in such a situation, I can tell you. I have never attended a meeting that covered so much ground, in which so little time was wasted in trying to figure out what people meant by what they said."

One does not have to go to Antwerp to find different backgrounds, points of view, or ways of speaking. Put sales, production, and finance people of any company together in the same room and you may see the same result. Knowing where to start, what questions to ask, and what to do is just as important if people all come from the same geographical area, or even from the same building.

An efficiently functioning team can be put together, but it must be *managed* into being. If you wish to develop an organization to its full potential, many things must be done in addition to teaching and installing a common approach and a common language for addressing management concerns. Assimilation of the concepts presented in this book is only the first step toward realizing their benefits. Continual, routine, shared use of the concepts must be planned for and made to happen by the organization if these benefits are to be achieved and maintained.

A Case History:
Using the Kepner-Tregoe Program

After a number of highly successful years in office, an executive in one company of a medium-sized conglomerate was promoted to the position of president and chief executive officer of the entire organization. The organization was stale. This fact was denied by no one. Under tight control by the previous president and major stockholders, with decision making confined almost exclusively to the top level, rifts and cliques had developed. One company within the conglomerate was played off against another to the detriment of productivity overall. The notion of mutual responsibility was unknown. Major problems had been ignored or swept under the rug for years. Now our executive was in the top position, not an altogether enviable one.

He contacted Kepner-Tregoe and explained that he wanted to build a management team around the use of our approaches. Five years earlier he had attended one of our workshops. He had believed then and ever since that the shared use of the ideas could do much to build teamwork among his organization's managers. Now he was able to put that belief to the test. He wanted managers at all levels—in all companies within the organization—to learn and use the Kepner-Tregoe approaches individually and together. He felt that this experience would enable the managers to begin to see themselves as managers of a single organization, not as vassals of a collection of fiefdoms.

Under his leadership the new president and his twenty-four senior executives were the first to learn and use the concepts. In the first week they analyzed nearly thirty situations, some of which had been avoided for years. Some were resolved; decisions were made to correct many more. The subordinates of this group of managers subsequently went through the same procedure. They learned to use the concepts, put them to work identifying and analyzing situations of major concern, and planned for continuing their analyses to the point of resolution. They then designated the next group of managers to follow suit. In this way, over a period of two months, eighty-four managers learned to use common approaches for addressing and resolving management concerns. New systems and procedures were established to support continuing use of these approaches.

By his actions, the new president said these things loudly and clearly and everyone in the organization heard them:

1. This is one organization.

2. By using common approaches to problems and decisions, we can work together cooperatively as parts of one organization.

3. Everyone will use these approaches, beginning with me.

4. You can think. Your knowledge and experience are important. You are in a position to use effectively the new approaches you have learned.

5. What you do with these approaches will have an important impact on the organization.

6. You are all valuable members of the management team.

The climate of that organization changed as nearly overnight as human nature allows. People learned to talk about problems that had not been discussed openly until then. They learned how to communicate their good ideas so that others would listen and understand why they were good. Through the use of systematic, commonly shared approaches, they solved many more problems and made better decisions than they had before. Who is to say how much of the success this conglomerate enjoyed over the years that followed was due to the use of systematic, commonly shared approaches, and how much to the sense of participation and pride engendered by the overall set of changes? The question is academic. One element without the other could not have produced the same result.

The president in this example let his people know he believed they could think, he wanted them-to express their ideas, he would listen, and they must listen to each other. He provided them with new conceptual tools so they could do a better job of working with available information. He led the way by using the new ideas himself. He established credibility for the new approaches by putting them to the test on real and important situations. He let people learn for themselves that the approaches worked in solving the kinds of concerns faced by the conglomerate and all its components.

- He made a *planned intervention* into his organization.

- He introduced the kinds of *major changes* he believed would do the most good.

- He introduced *a new idea* to his people: I value your ability to think, to come up with good ideas, to express those ideas individually and cooperatively.

- He introduced *a means by which thinking could be coordinated and channeled*. The *climate of cooperation and teamwork followed and was a result of the intervention*.

- Finally, he modified the systems and procedures of the organization to *provide support* for the continuing use of the new ideas.

The new president did not set out to build teamwork or group cohesiveness as desirable things that would somehow improve the operation of the company. He did not try to heal the scars of past in-fighting and conflict. He let teamwork, cohesiveness, and mutual respect grow out of the experience of working together with common guidelines and procedures. He made sure the results of that experience—problems accurately identified and resolved, decisions well formulated and successfully implemented—were recognized and rewarded.

Conditions for Workable Change

For years social scientists have said that humans resist change—and so they do. But they resist only those changes they do not understand, are suspicious of, or consider to be against their interests. Humans embrace change that seems good for them or good for the world they live in and care about.

A new idea or a new expectation, in itself, will seldom bring about change. On the other hand, change can be very attractive if it is the product of a new idea or expectation that appears to be in the best interests of the people who are expected to adopt it, if it is accompanied by the means for its fulfillment, and if it results in recognition and approval. To improve an organization, we must introduce good ideas, establish the means for making them work, and provide a visible payoff for the effort involved.

No organization can reach its full potential unless it promotes and enjoys the coordination of productive activities among its members. The more complex the activities of the organization, the more need there is for coordination if the organization is to flourish. No one knows it all anymore. Teamwork is an increasingly critical element in organizational success; fortunately, it is not difficult to achieve. But teamwork must be managed into existence through experiences that are capable of producing teamwork.

Four Basic Patterns of Thinking

Teamwork can be managed into existence by teaching people to use consciously and cooperatively four basic patterns of thinking they already use unconsciously and individually. These four basic patterns of thinking are reflected in the four kinds of questions managers ask every day:

WHAT'S GOING ON?

WHY DID THIS HAPPEN?

WHICH COURSE OF ACTION SHOULD WE TAKE?

WHAT LIES AHEAD?

WHAT'S GOING ON? begs for *clarification*. It asks for a sorting out, a breaking down, a key to the map of current events, a means of achieving and maintaining control. It reflects the pattern of thinking that enables us to impose order where all had been disorder, uncertainty, or confusion. It enables us to establish priorities and decide when and how to take actions that make good sense and produce good results.

WHY DID THIS HAPPEN? indicates the need for *cause-and-effect* thinking, the second basic pattern. It is the pattern that enables us to move from observing the effect of a problem to understanding its cause so that we can take appropriate actions to correct the problem or lessen its effects.

WHICH COURSE OF ACTION SHOULD WE TAKE? implies that some *choice* must be made. This third basic pattern of thinking enables us to decide on the course of action most likely to accomplish a particular goal.

WHAT LIES AHEAD? looks into the future. We use this fourth basic pattern of thinking when we attempt to assess the problem that *might* happen, the decision that *might* be necessary next month, next year, or in five years.

Four kinds of questions. Four basic patterns of thinking. Of course people ask other questions and think in other patterns. Nevertheless, every productive activity that takes place within an organization is related to one of these four basic patterns.

In the Beginning: Thinking Patterns for Survival

The four basic patterns of thinking have not altered substantially since emergence of the human race. The patterns are universal and universally applicable to any situation. Over millions of years, through natural selection these neurological structures—the patterns of thinking, response, and behavior that promoted survival—tended to be preserved and passed on; patterns with low survival value dropped out. Humans became adaptive (problem solving) in their way of life. The elements that made possible those patterns of thinking became part of human nature.

The ability to ask and answer the questions "What's going on?" "Why?" "Which?" and "What lies ahead?" made civilization possible. By accumulating answers to these questions, humans learned how to deal with complexity, how to discover why things are as they are, how to make good choices, and how to anticipate the future.

Survival was guaranteed by the ability to use these patterns, to think clearly, and to communicate with one another for a common purpose. To most people "survival" implies a teetering on the edge of death, a probable fall one way or the other, and the intervention of something that will determine the direction of the fall. In mankind's distant past, when survival concerned the individual alone, this may indeed have been true. But survival depended more often upon the actions of a group of individuals working together, perhaps as a hunting or food-gathering group. The group became a team by working together. Teamwork ensured a food supply for everyone. Teamwork ensured shelter, protection, and a basis for living in a brutally competitive world. There was a place for physical strength, but brains combined with strength counted for far more.

Pattern 1: Assessing and Clarifying

For our earliest ancestors, the most important of the four basic patterns of thinking was the one that enabled them to assess, clarify, sort out, and impose order on a confusing situation. Humans could separate a complex situation into its components, decide what had to be done, and determine when, how, and by whom it would be done. They could set priorities and delegate tasks. This was an integral part of human adaptability—the condition that permits us to change based on an assessment of "what's going on." Animals adapt and change in response to external changes, but human adaptation is a chosen behavior resulting from such assessment. Twenty thousand years ago, the answers to "What's going on?" may have pointed to a slowly vanishing food source, a recurring flood, or an influx of animal pests. In response, humans took the steps necessary for survival: move to a new location, alter eating habits, adopt better hunting practices. In short, this fundamental pattern of thinking enabled humans to prevail in a variety of surroundings and against an array of profoundly adverse conditions.

Pattern 2: Cause and Effect

The second basic pattern of thinking—the one that permits us to relate an event to its outcome, a cause to its effect—gave early man the ability to assign meaning to what he observed. The earliest humans did not understand such natural events as birth, illness, and death, or the rising and setting of the sun. That understanding came much later through the accumulation, contemplation, and communication of observations about their world. It was the refinement of cause-and-effect thinking that enabled humans to move beyond mere reaction to their environment, to make use of the environment instead of being forever at its mercy.

Small children constantly ask, "But *why?*" They are exhibiting this basic thinking pattern: the desire to know why things are as they are and why they happen as they do. This desire is so basic that even an inaccurate explanation of a puzzling fact is preferable to none at all. Early man was satisfied with an explanation of a universe that revolved around the activities of supernatural beings. It was far preferable to no explanation at all for such readily perceived phenomena as the changing nature of a star-filled sky. Even today we have relatively few answers to the gigantic puzzle of the universe, but the answers we do have are comforting.

The thinking pattern we use to relate cause and effect is as basic and natural as the pattern we use to assess and clarify complex situations. Both enable us to survive, flourish, and maintain a true measure of control over our environment.

Pattern 3: Making Choices

The third basic pattern of thinking enables us to make reasoned choices. It is the pattern that permitted early man to decide whether to continue the hunt all night or wait until morning, hide in this cave or that tree, camp on this or that side of the river. Productive, coherent action—as opposed to simple reaction to the event of the moment—depends on a sound basis for choice. In a hostile environment populated with larger, stronger, and faster creatures, random action too often could have only one end for early man, and that sudden. The development of sophistication in the making of choices, along with goal setting and consideration of the consequences of one action as opposed to another, meant that humans could sometimes eat tigers instead of vice versa.

The choice-making pattern gives rise to three major activities:

- Determination of purpose (to what end the choice is being made).

- Consideration of available options (how best to fulfill the purpose).

- Assessment of the relative risks of available options (which action is likely to be safest or most productive).

When faced with a choice, we are likely to spend most of our time and thought on only one of these three activities. But whatever the balance, however complex the choice, these three factors determine the kinds of choices humans have always made and continue to make.

Pattern 4: Anticipating the Future

The fourth basic pattern of thinking enables us to look into the future to see the good and bad it may hold. This ability to imagine and construe the future, even a little way ahead and that imperfectly, gave our ancestors a tremendous advantage. It permitted them to anticipate the storm and the snake, the starvation of winter, the thirst of summer. Future-oriented thinking was made possible largely by the superior development of cause-and-effect thinking (the second basic pattern described above). Humans learned to apply their knowledge of cause-and-effect relationships: of what *had happened,* and why, to what *could happen* and what the future *might hold.* They learned to take actions in the present against the possible and probable negative events of the future.

Although preventive action is as old as the human race, the thinking pattern that produces this action is less successful than our other patterns. Unfortunately, the future carries less urgency than the present. Early man learned to keep some of the food of summer against the ravages of winter—but the supply was rarely adequate. The importance of the future tiger, the future fire, or future starvation was small compared with the immediacy of the tiger five yards away, the threat of fire visibly approaching, or the reality of imminent starvation. Even today we face the unfulfilled potential of this fourth basic pattern of thinking: the ability to plan ahead, to take action today against the negative events of tomorrow.

Basic Patterns of Thinking in the Organizational Context

Kepner-Tregoe has developed four basic rational processes for using and sharing information about organizational concerns. These processes are systematic procedures for making the best possible use of the four patterns of thinking. This is why the

Kepner-Tregoe processes are universally applicable regardless of cultural setting, regardless of the content against which they are applied. Whether managers are Japanese, Canadian, or Brazilian, they are all equipped—as a result of common human experiences—with identical, unchangeable patterns of thinking. It is only content that changes.

Situation Appraisal

The rational process based on the first thinking pattern is called *Situation Appraisal*. It deals with the question "What's going on?" and with assessing and clarifying situations, sorting things out, breaking down complex situations into manageable components, and maintaining control of events.

When a management situation occurs, the available information is usually a confusion of the relevant and the irrelevant, the important and the inconsequential. Before anything reasonable or productive can be done, the confused situation must be sorted out so that its components can be seen in perspective. Priorities must be set and actions delegated. There must be some means of keeping track of information as old situations are resolved and new ones take their place.

Situation Appraisal is designed to identify problems to be solved, decisions to be made, and future events to be analyzed and planned. Therefore, we must understand the rational processes applicable to these areas before studying the techniques and procedures of Situation Appraisal itself. For this reason Situation Appraisal is presented in Chapter Seven, following the explanation of the three remaining rational processes: Problem Analysis, Decision Analysis, and Potential Problem Analysis.

Problem Analysis

The second rational process, called *Problem Analysis,* is based on the cause-and-effect thinking pattern. It enables us to accurately identify, describe, analyze, and resolve a situation in which *something has gone wrong without explanation.* It gives us a methodical means to extract essential information from a troublesome situation and set aside irrelevant, confusing information.

Problem Analysis is explained in Chapter Two, and examples of its use are presented in Chapter Three.

Decision Analysis

The third rational process, based on the choice-making pattern of thinking, is called *Decision Analysis*. Using this process, we can stand back from a decision situation and evaluate its three components. We can analyze the reasons for making the decision and examine its purpose. We can analyze the available options for achieving that purpose. We can analyze the relative risks of each alternative. From this balanced picture of the situation, we can then make the wisest and safest choice—the one that has emerged after careful consideration of all the factors.

Decision Analysis is explained in Chapter Four, and examples of its use are presented in Chapter Five.

Potential Problem Analysis

The fourth rational process is based on our concern with future events—with what *might* be and what *could* happen. We call it *Potential Problem Analysis*. A potential problem exists when we can foresee possible trouble in a given situation. No one knows for sure that trouble will develop, but no one can guarantee that it will not. This process uses what we know or can safely assume in order to avoid possible negative consequences in the future. It is based on the idea that thinking and acting beforehand to prevent a problem is more efficient than solving a problem that has been allowed to develop. This rational process enables an organization to take an active hand in shaping its future.

Chapter Six deals with the ways organizations have used Potential Problem Analysis to reduce the number and severity of their problems.

The Rise, Fall, and Rise Again of Teamwork

All humans have the inherent capacity to think in terms of Situation Appraisal, Problem Analysis, Decision Analysis, and Potential Problem Analysis. These processes are basic and natural. Unfortunately, they cannot be put to work automatically, used equally well by all humans, or used on a shared basis. Why should this be so?

Every person has a personal, idiosyncratic way of understanding, handling, and communicating such things as cause-and-effect relationships and choice-making. Some people develop better ways than others. Some may be only moderately skilled in, say, cause-and-effect thinking but exceptionally good at communicating their conclusions. (They may be more successful than others who are more skilled but less communicative.) The way a person thinks can be deduced only by observing that person's behavior and paying careful attention to his or her conclusions. What information was used and how it was used remain invisible. "I don't see how you could arrive at that" is our ordinary way of expressing the fact that thinking is an inside job.

So we have a two-fold need, complicated by the fact that we are often unaware even of our own thinking patterns. The actual *level of skill in thinking*—about problems, decisions, and all other organizational concerns—*needs to be as high as it can be*. That level of skill rises when people have grasped the techniques of rational processes and have learned to apply their basic thinking patterns to management concerns. That's the easy part. *It is more difficult for people to learn to think together.* How can we achieve teamwork in an activity as individual and internal as thinking?

Teamwork in the use of patterns of thinking does not just happen. As discussed earlier, it must be contrived, consciously planned, or unconsciously fostered through the closeness and visibility of the team members. A group may become a team of sorts simply by working together on a particular task for a long enough time. They may come to understand each other's roles in a common task. They may come to appreciate each other's ways of thinking and learn to accommodate to individual idiosyncrasies in the way information is used. Although a workable set of effective and appropriate compromises may emerge from this context, this group is not yet the full-scale, multipurpose team that can truly share in the thinking process.

Hunting and Gathering:
Models of Superior Teamwork

We can gain insight into what is useful in today's organizations by speculating on the achievement and consequences of teamwork exhibited by our earliest ancestors. Teamwork is perceived as a precious commodity today, and the earliest humans had it down pat.

For early man, available information was largely visual: tracks, signs, and indications could be mutually observed and pointed out. Hunting and food-gathering groups were small— probably fifteen to forty people of all ages. The young learned from the old through intimate contact and close observation. Old and young pooled their intellectual resources by talking about what they saw. They thought aloud—a characteristic typical of people who live together closely. In this way they acquired commonly understood meanings for their words. Their language became expressive of detail, of fine distinctions of form, color, texture, and of thoughts and feelings. They developed few abstract terms. The languages of hunting and gathering groups that survive today retain these characteristics, suggesting how life's business probably was conducted by early man. Although there is no difference between their mental processes and ours, early man's need for communication led to a language rich in concrete, literal words that were open to verification and that had explicit definitions within a shared reality.

With a common experience of their environment and a common set of terms to describe it, the members of a hunting team functioned more as a single coordinated body than any comparable modern group. The leader was the most proficient and skillful but there was no need for him to give orders and directions. Everyone understood what was to be done, who could do it best, and how to mesh individual efforts into a concerted whole. Entire vocabularies were committed to sign language to preserve silence. Hundreds of words could be expressed by formalized gestures instantly and commonly understood.

It is little wonder that hunting and gathering people were able to achieve such a high order of coordination and teamwork in their activities. It was as though they carried on-board headbone computers commonly programmed with a single shared set of routines and instructions. With these computers so closely aligned, even a little information was sufficient to trigger a common understanding among all those who received it: They knew what the information meant and what was to be done. There was little ambiguity or uncertainty in the treatment of and response to an input. Success and survival depended upon everyone's getting the same message at the same time. Teamwork among humans probably reached its highest point of development with the hunting peoples, immediately before the advent of agriculture. This teamwork was made possible by possession of a common language to express and share a common way of thinking.

The domestication of plants and animals doomed the hunting life, No longer was it necessary for the members of a band to think and exist in so parallel a fashion. Now there was specialization of function. Groups became larger, and diverse social and political units appeared. Now there was room for different beliefs and behavior. Gone was the economic uncertainty of hunting and gathering, but gone also was the closeness such a life imposed. The intense teamwork of the hunting group disappeared forever; the luxury of individual thought and individual interpretation of ideas had arrived.

Applying the Model:
Needs of the Modern Organization

No one in his right mind wants to go back to the days of hunting and gathering. But it would be tremendously valuable if we could recapture that ability to work together with even a fraction of that efficiency to deal better with modern problem situations. Now, through contrivance and planning, we *can* recapture that ability and channel it to meet the needs of the modern organization.

This is not to say that the organizational team will somehow represent a modern hunting group armed with ballpoint pens instead of bows and arrows. Hunters' ways of thinking were totally aligned, and their lives were totally aligned. What is required today is not total teamwork in all aspects of life; rather, it is a selective, functional teamwork that can be turned on when needed, limited to those activities where it will be most productive. What is required is teamwork that can be summoned to handle organizational problems yet leave team members free to act as individuals in all other respects.

We need an approach that can be invoked and shared when we need answers to specific questions, regardless of content: the "What's going on?" that applies orderliness to complexity and confusion; the "Why?" of any set of circumstances in which the cause-and-effect relationship is obscure; the "Which?" of a situation in which one course of action must be adopted in favor of others; the "What lies ahead?" that must be thoughtfully considered in order to protect and nurture the organization's future.

We need the kinds of accurate communication and common understanding that prevailed in the hunting bands. These must be modernized, selectively adapted to current conditions, and directed toward the critical functions of organizational activity where teamwork is most essential.

All of this can be done. It is just what was done by the company president who spoke earlier in this chapter. He brought into his organization a common language and common approaches for using the four basic patterns of thinking that produce orderliness, resolve problems, make good choices, and protect against future threats. His people learned to share this language and use these approaches. Their acceptance of his new and different *modus operandi* came as a result of their own experience.

The new, common language they learned was not a long list of jargon that required a month to memorize. It consisted of down-to-earth words and phrases that convey an exact meaning to everyone exposed to that language. Such sentences as "I'm not sure you really understood what I meant" were heard less and less frequently. The new, common approaches worked when they were applied to real situations within the organization. The individual payoff for adopting the new behavior was great; the organizational payoff was greater. The people of the organization soon were equipped to act as a team in the fullest sense of the word.

Rational Management

Such results begin to occur only after planning and plain hard work. Rational management, which means *making full use of the thinking ability of the people in an organization,* is a continuing process. Use of the ideas—and their benefits—will eventually fade out if they are not continually used and reinforced.

Rational Management aims at major change and therefore demands major commitment. The four rational processes we will describe in the next several chapters constitute an explicit, logical system that can have a far-reaching impact within an organization. But this system cannot be introduced by half-heartedly sprinkling a few ideas and suggestions among a random mix of the organization's people in the hope that something good will happen. We must identify the significant people within the organization, for they should be the first to learn and use the new ideas. We must identify their subordinates and the people who provide them with information. We must identify those who will implement the conclusions that come out of the use of the ideas. In short it is imperative to pinpoint *all the people within an organization who make things happen.* The objective is to move the organization closer to its full potential. This can be done only by introducing teamwork based on the continuing *conscious* use of common approaches expressed in a simple, common language and directed toward resolution of an organization's important concerns.

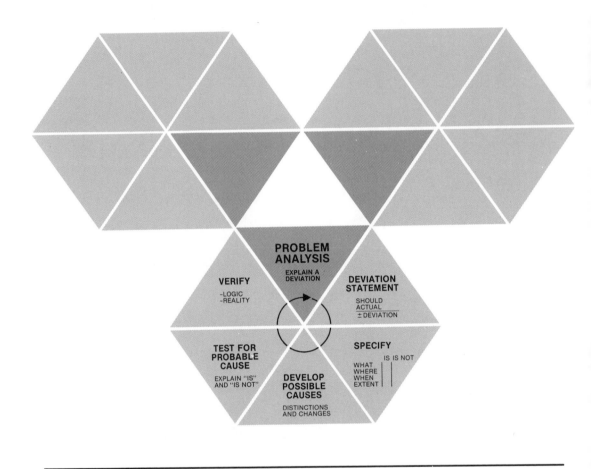

CHAPTER 2

Problem Analysis

Introduction:
The Conditions and Skills of Problem Solving

People like to solve problems. While people in an organization enjoy the rewards that go with success, they also enjoy the process that produces success. Regardless of their organizational level, they not only will accept but they will seek problem-solving opportunities as long as four conditions exist:

- They must possess the skills needed to solve the problems that arise on their jobs.

- They must experience success in using those skills.

- They must be rewarded for successfully resolving their problems.

- They must not fear failure.

The converse is equally true. People will avoid problem-solving situations when they are unsure of how to solve their problems, when they do not experience success after trying to solve a problem, when they feel that their efforts are not appreciated, and when they sense that they have less to lose either by doing nothing or by shifting responsibility. This chapter is concerned with the first condition: *the skills that make problem-solving behavior possibie.* The other conditions for habitual, successful problem solving will be discussed in subsequent chapters.

Problem Analysis provides the skills needed *to explain any situation in which an expected level of performance is not being achieved* and *in which the cause of the unacceptable performance is unknown.* If *any situation* seems too strong a phrase, remember that we are concerned with *the way in which information is used to approach deviations in performance.* These deviations may appear in the performance of people or the performance of systems, policies, or equipment—that is, anything in the work environment that may deviate from expected performance with no known cause. As long as this structure applies, the techniques of Problem Analysis also apply.

In this chapter we will explain and demonstrate Problem Analysis by examining a problem that occurred in a production plant owned by one of our clients. We have selected this problem as a case vehicle because it is concrete and easily understood, therefore ideal for introducing the techniques of Problem Analysis. In Chapter Three we will describe the use of these techniques in a variety of industries, at differing organizational levels, and over a wide spectrum of problem situations.

Cause and Effect

Problem solving requires cause-and-effect thinking, one of the four basic thinking patterns described in Chapter One. A problem is the visible effect of a cause that resides somewhere in the past. We must relate the effect we observe to its exact cause. Only then can we be sure of taking appropriate corrective action—action that can correct the problem and keep it from recurring.

Everyone has experienced the solved problem that turns out not to have been solved at all. A simple example is the car that stalls in traffic, goes into the shop for costly repair, and then stalls again on the way home. If the cause of the stalling is a worn-out distributor and the action taken is a readjustment of the carburetor, then the car will continue to stall. Superior problem solving is not the result of knowing all the things that *can* produce a particular effect and then choosing a corrective action directed at the most frequently observed cause. Yet this is the way most people approach problems on the job. Problem Analysis is a *systematic problem-solving process.* It does not reject the value of experience or of technical knowledge. Rather, it helps us to make the best use of that experience and knowledge. Our objectivity about a situation is often sacrificed under pressure. When a quick solution to a problem is required, it is too easy to rely on memories of what happened in the past, on the solution that was successful once before, or on the remedy that corrected an apparently similar problem. This is the most common approach to problem solving, and problem solving by extrapolation from past events to current events is a tough habit to break despite its relatively poor payoff in appropriate, lasting corrective actions. A chief purpose of this chapter and the next is to demonstrate that the habit can be broken. Through the experiences of people in our client organizations, we will show that the effort required to adopt a systematic approach to problem solving is small in light of the results that follow.

The Criteria That Define a Problem

The following are typical examples of problems. They meet our definition of a problem because in each one an expected level of performance is not being achieved, and the cause of the unacceptable performance is unknown.

> "From the day we introduced the computer, we've had nothing but trouble in getting our inventories to balance. I just don't understand it."

> "Emory Jackson was referred to us as an outstanding engineer, but he certainly hasn't fulfilled expectations in this department."

> "Our Number Eleven paper machine never produces more than 80% of its design capacity no matter what we try."

> "Some days we meet our schedules without any trouble. Other days we can't meet them at all. There just doesn't seem to be any good reason for the discrepancy."

> "The system worked well for months. Then, in the middle of the morning three weeks ago, it went dead. It's still dead and we don't have the slightest idea of what happened."

Despite disparities in content, seriousness, and scope of these five examples, they all indicate a degree of performance failure, confusion or total lack of understanding about its cause, and the need to find a correct explanation.

There are other kinds of problem situations that do not meet our specific definition. For example:

> "There is no way we can meet our deadline on the project with our present staff and no way we can get authorization to bring on anyone new. This is a serious problem. . . ."

This statement represents the need for one or more decisions. It does *not* represent a deviation between expected and actual performance that is of *unknown* cause. In this example, resolution will consist not of an explanation as to why the situation arose but of a choice: Those concerned must identify some course of action that can produce satisfactory results under less than optimal conditions.

Compromises will probably be identified. Objectives for meeting the goal may have to be reviewed, reshuffled, or altered. Any number of potential actions may be considered. But the cause of the difficulty is known all too well. Decision Analysis, which is presented in Chapters Four and Five, is useful for resolution of this kind of dilemma. A decision requires answers to the questions "How?" "Which?" and "To what purpose?" A problem always requires an answer to the question "Why?"

The Structure of a Problem

A performance standard is achieved when all conditions required for acceptable performance are operating as they should. This is true for everything in the work environment: people, systems, departments, and pieces of equipment. If there is an alteration in one or more of these conditions—that is, if some kind of change occurs—then it is possible that performance will alter too. That change may be for the better or worse. Sometimes conditions improve, positive changes occur, and things go better than expected. But an unexpected rise in performance seldom triggers the same urgent response as an unexpected decline. The more serious the effect of the decline, the more pressure there is to find the cause and do something about it.

We may visualize the structure of a problem as shown in Figure 1.

Figure 1.

Structure of a Problem

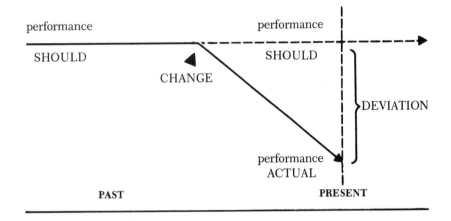

If performance once met the SHOULD and no longer does, then a change has occurred. At the outset of problem solving, we do not know exactly what that change consisted of or when it occurred.

The search for cause usually entails a search for a specific change that has caused a decline in performance. In some cases, however, a negative deviation in performance—a so-called Day One Deviation—has always existed. An example is an equipment unit that "never was any good *from the day it came on line. . . .*" In this instance, using our terminology, ACTUAL has *always* been below SHOULD. This kind of problem can be visualized as shown in Figure 2.

Figure 2.

Structure of a Day One Problem

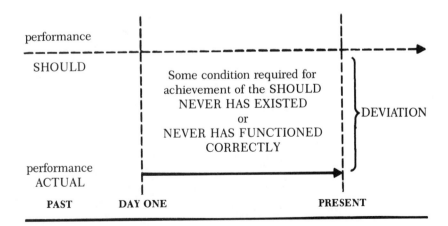

The Techniques of Problem Analysis

Both kinds of problems—a current deviation from formerly acceptable performance and a performance that has never met expectations—can be approached through the techniques of Problem Analysis.

The techniques are divided into these major categories:

1. Definition of the problem.

2. Description of the problem in four dimensions: Identity, Location, Timing, and Magnitude.

3. Extraction of key information in the four dimensions to generate possible causes.

4. Testing for most probable cause.

5. Verification of the true cause.

The History of a Problem

The history of our true case vehicle is a necessary prelude to demonstration of the Problem Analysis techniques. The Case of the Leaking Soybean Oil Filter may never make a best-selling mystery but, as with most real-life mysteries, to the people who had to live with it, explain it, and correct it, it was of far more interest than any best seller. Although Problem Analysis was used *after* the explanation had been arrived at (quite accidentally), it demonstrated to the people who had worked inefficiently and unsuccessfully on the problem for several days that a systematic process of investigation would have produced the correct explanation within a matter of hours.

Our client is a major food processor. One of the company plants produces oil from corn and soybeans. The five units that filter the oil are located in one building. On the day the problem was first observed, a foreman rushed into his supervisor's office: "Number One Filter is leaking. There's oil all over the floor of the filter house."

The foreman guessed that the leak was caused by valves loosening up from vibration. This had happened once before. "Number One sits right next to the main feedwater pump and gets shaken up more than the other four filters." A mechanic tried to find the leak but couldn't tell much because the oil had already been cleaned up. The lid fastener looked all right. After examining pipes, valves, and the walls of the filter chamber, the mechanic concluded that the oil had spilled from another source.

The next day there was more oil. Another mechanic traced the leak to the cleanout hatch but that didn't help much. Why should the cleanout hatch leak? It looked perfectly all right. Just to be on the safe side, he replaced the gasket even though it looked new. The hatch continued to leak. "Maintenance people just aren't closing it tight enough after they clean it out," someone volunteered. "There are a couple of new guys on maintenance here since the shifts were changed around last month. I wonder if they're using a torque wrench like they're supposed to. This happened to us once before because somebody didn't use a torque wrench." No one could say for sure.

The next day an operator slipped on the oil-slick floor and hurt his back. The cleanup task was becoming more than irksome, according to some outspoken comments overheard by the foreman. A few people began grumbling about promises made at the last safety meeting about improving conditions in the filter house. Two days later the plant manager got wind of the situation, called in the supervisor and the foreman, and made it clear that he expected a solution to the oil mess problem within the day.

That afternoon someone asked, "How come this gasket on Number One Filter has square corners? They always used to have rounded corners." A quick check of the filters revealed that the other four filters still had round-cornered gaskets. This led to the discovery that the square-cornered gasket on Number One Filter had been installed the evening before the leaking was first noticed. It had come from a new lot purchased from a new supplier who charged 10¢ less per unit. This led to the question "How can they sell them for 10¢ less?" and to the subsequent observation "Because they're no damned good."

The new gasket was inspected and compared with the old gaskets. It was easy to see that the new one was thinner and uneven. It was equally clear that this gasket was never designed to be used on this kind of filter unit. It would always leak. It should never have been installed. Additional gaskets were purchased from the original supplier and installed. The leaking stopped.

Looking back at the problem, a few people said they had had ideas about its cause but couldn't explain how the causes they thought of could produce the effect. Actions taken before the problem was solved had been based on experience, on similar problems in the past, on standard operating procedures, and on hunches. The faulty gasket had even been replaced with an identical (and therefore equally useless) one "just to be on the safe side."

Sometimes we stumble on the cause of a problem. Sometimes we take an action that just happens to correct the effect although the cause is never explained fully. In the latter case—cause unknown and the action that solved the problem, one of many taken at the same time—a recurrence of the effect will mean that all those same actions may have to be repeated to ensure correction!

At other times the cause is neither discovered nor stumbled upon, and *no* action corrects the effect. An interim, or holding, action must be devised so that the operation can live with the problem until its true cause is found—or until problem-solving roulette produces a winning number. More often than managers would like, that happy accident never occurs. Interim action gradually becomes standard operating procedure.

The Case of the Leaking Soybean Oil Filter was reconstructed as a Problem Analysis for plant employees who were learning to use the techniques. It worked very well to make the point that the roulette approach, however familiar, produces frustration and misunderstanding more often than results. Motivation to use a systematic approach grew as soon as the employees recognized that they had worked for several days in a mess that could have been corrected permanently in a matter of hours.

The Process of Problem Analysis

The remainder of this chapter is a step-by-step demonstration of Problem Analysis, exactly as it could have been used when the leaking oil filter problem was first observed.

1. Definition of the Problem, or The Deviation Statement

We must first define a problem exactly before we can describe, analyze, and explain it. We define it with the *deviation statement,* or name of the problem. It is important to state this name precisely because all the work to follow—all the description, analysis, and explanation we will undertake—will be directed at correcting the problem *as it has been named.* The name of this problem is "Number One Filter Leaking Oil."

This seems obvious enough. But suppose we had worded the deviation statement "Oil on the Filter House Floor." Any way you look at it, oil on the floor is certainly a deviation from SHOULD. Yet it is of known cause and all that a logical analysis can produce as an explanation is "Number One Filter Leaking Oil." This is where we want to begin our search, not end it.

However simple or complex a problem may seem at the outset, it is always worth a minute or two to ask, "Can the effect of this problem *as we have described it* in the deviation statement be explained now?" If it can, as in "Oil on the Floor," we must back up to the point at which we can no longer explain the deviation statement. Vague or generalized deviation statements that begin with such phrases as "Low productivity on . . ." or "Sub-standard performance by . . ." must be reworded into specific deviation statements that name one object or kind of object, and one malfunction or kind of malfunction for which we wish to discover and explain cause.

It is tempting to combine two or more deviations in a single problem-solving effort or to try to bunch a bevy of seemingly related problems into one overall problem. Nearly everyone has attended meetings during which two or more distinct problems were tied ankle to ankle in a kind of problem-solving sack race. This procedure is almost always inefficient and unproductive.

2. Description of the Problem in Four Dimensions: Identity, Location, Timing, and Magnitude

Once we have a precise deviation statement, the next step in Problem Analysis is to describe the problem in detail, or *specify* it in its four dimensions:

IDENTITY	— what it is we're trying to explain
LOCATION	— where we observe it
TIMING	— when it occurs
MAGNITUDE	— how serious, how extensive it is

All obtainable information about any problem will fall within one of these four dimensions. Within each we ask *specifying questions* that will flesh out our description of the effect of the problem and give us exactly the kinds of information that will be most useful for analysis.

| IDENTITY | WHAT is the unit that is malfunctioning? | Number 1 Filter |
| | WHAT is the malfunction? | Leaking oil |

LOCATION	WHERE is the malfunction observed (geographically)?	Northeast corner of filter house
	WHERE on the unit is the malfunction observed?	At the cleanout hatch
TIMING	WHEN was the malfunction first observed?	Three days ago, at the start of shift
	WHEN has it been observed since?	Continuously, on all shifts
	WHEN in the operating cycle of the unit is the malfunction first observed?	As soon as oil goes into filter, at start of shift
MAGNITUDE	WHAT is the extent of the problem?	Five to ten gallons of oil leaked per shift
	HOW MANY units are affected?	Only Number 1 (as above)
	HOW MUCH of any one unit is affected?	N/A

In the dimension of Magnitude, the response to "How much of any one unit is affected?" is N/A—not applicable. This illustrates the fact that every problem is unique and its informational context reflects that uniqueness. As a result, one or more of the specifying questions may not produce useful information. *Nevertheless we ask.* We always attempt to answer every question. Skipping questions that probably don't matter destroys the objectivity we are working so diligently to maintain.

Given only a few variations in wording, any problem can be described by answering the specifying questions. Suppose that the object of our concern is not a unit but a system or part or all of a function. When we are dealing with a human performance problem, we must alter the questions to reflect the fact that we are observing people and behavior, not units and malfunctions. There are other variations on the basic techniques. When we are working with human performance, we usually need to use a combination of rational process ideas—not only those found within the Problem Analysis process. For these reasons we will deal separately with human performance, in Chapter Eight, after explaining all the rational processes.

Once we have described our problem in the four dimensions of Identity, Location, Timing, and Magnitude, we have exactly one-half the total specification we want. It is the second half that will render it a useful tool for analysis.

IS and IS NOT: A Basis of Comparison

We know that our problem IS "Number One Filter Leaking Oil." What would we gain by identifying a unit that COULD BE leaking but IS NOT? Or the locations at which oil COULD BE observed to leak but IS NOT? Such data would give us what we need to conduct an analysis: *a basis of comparison.* Once we have identified COULD BE but IS NOT data, we will also be able to identify the peculiar factors that isolate our problem: exactly what it is, where it is observed, when it is observed, and its extent or magnitude. These peculiar factors will lead us closer to the problem's cause.

Suppose for a moment that you have two identical potted plants growing in your office. One thrives but the other does not. If you take the wilting plant out of the office and ask someone about the probable cause for its sorry appearance, you will get any number of educated guesses. But if the same person observes that two identical plants in your office have not been receiving identical treatment (the thriving plant is on a sunny window sill and the wilting one is in a dim corner), the speculations as to cause will be immediate and more accurate than they could have been without a basis of comparison. *Regardless of the content of a problem, nothing is more conducive to sound analysis than some relevant basis of comparison.*

In Problem Analysis we conduct the search for bases of comparison in all four dimensions of the specification. We will now repeat our deviation statement and the specifying questions and answers, and add a third column called Closest Logical Comparison. In this column we will establish the problem as it COULD BE but IS NOT in terms of identity, location, timing, and magnitude. Let us see how this works out in Figure 3, shown on pages 44–45.

Note that the second specifying question in the Identity dimension does not suggest a close, logical comparison. It would not make any sense to list some other problem that might be observed but is not. In this case leaking oil cannot be compared usefully with any other specific malfunction. The decision as to what is close and what is logical must rest with the judgment of the problem solver or the team. In many cases it is extremely important to identify the malfunction that COULD BE but IS NOT in order to narrow the scope of the search for cause. Each Problem Analysis is unique to the content of each problem.

Once we have identified bases of comparison in all four dimensions, we are able to isolate key distinguishing features of the problem. It is as if we had been describing the outlines of a shadow. With the completion of the IS NOT data in our specification, the outlines begin to suggest the components capable of having cast the shadow.

Figure 3.   **Deviation Statement:**

	SPECIFYING QUESTIONS
IDENTITY	WHAT is the unit with the malfunction?
	WHAT is the malfunction?
LOCATION	WHERE is the malfunction observed (geographically)?
	WHERE on the unit is the malfunction observed?
TIMING	WHEN was the malfunction first observed?
	WHEN has it been observed since?
	WHEN in the operating cycle of the unit is the malfunction first observed?
MAGNITUDE	WHAT is the EXTENT of the malfunction?
	HOW MANY units are affected?
	HOW MUCH of any one unit is affected?

3. *Extraction of Key Information in the Problem's Four Dimensions to Generate Possible Causes*

Distinctions

Number One Filter leaks; Numbers Two through Five might . . .but do not. What is *distinctive* about the Number One Filter *compared with the others*? What stands out?

  As the question "What is distinctive?" is applied to all four dimensions of a problem, our analysis begins to reveal important clues to the cause of the problem—*clues*, not answers or explanations. Let us return for a moment to the wilted plant in a dim corner of the office. With a basis of comparison (the identical plant that thrives on a sunny window sill), we quickly

Number One Filter Leaking Oil

PERFORMANCE DEVIATION	CLOSEST LOGICAL COMPARISON
IS Number 1 Filter	COULD BE but IS NOT Numbers 2–5
IS leaking oil	(No logical comparison)
IS observed at northeast corner of filter house	COULD BE but IS NOT observed at other filter locations
IS observed at the cleanout hatch	COULD BE but IS NOT observed at valves, pipes, locking mechanism
IS first observed three days ago	COULD BE but IS NOT observed before three days ago
IS observed continually, all shifts	COULD BE but IS NOT observed when unit is not in use
IS first observed as soon as oil goes into filter at start of shift	COULD BE but IS NOT first observed at a time later on in shift
IS 5–10 gallons of oil leaked per shift	COULD BE but IS NOT less than 5, more than 10 gallons per shift
IS Number 1 Filter only	COULD BE but IS NOT Filters 2–5
N/A	N/A

see a factor that is highly suggestive of cause. We said earlier that anyone observing this difference of treatment is likely to offer a quick opinion about the plant's wilted appearance. This natural cause-and-effect thinking pattern we all employ ensures that we all use this kind of reasoning when confronted with a problem *provided that we observe a distinction that taps something in our experience.*

At this point in Problem Analysis we identify the distinctions that characterize the problem in terms of its identity, location, timing, and magnitude when compared with the identity, location, timing, and magnitude that *might* characterize it but *do not*. We will now repeat all the columns we have already developed and add a column headed WHAT IS DISTINCTIVE ABOUT. . . . (This is shown in Figure 4, pages 48–49.) The question we ask to elicit distinctions is this: "What is distinctive about (the IS data) when compared with (the IS NOT data)?"

The four dimensions of a specification yield distinctions of differing quantity and quality. One or more dimensions frequently yield no distinctions at all. Obviously, the goal is quality: strong clues, outstanding features of the IS data.

Changes

In *Figure 1. Structure of a Problem,* on page 37, the arrowhead indicates change at a point between past acceptable performance—at which time the SHOULD was being achieved—and the current, unacceptable ACTUAL level of performance.

Managers who may never have heard of Problem Analysis know that a decline in a formerly acceptable performance suggests that something has changed; common sense tells them to look for that change. But such a search can be extremely frustrating when the manager is faced with an array of changes—changes that are known and planned, changes that are unforeseen, which continually creep into every operation.

Instead of searching through this mass of changes to find that one, elusive problem-solving change, we examine the one, small clearly defined area in which we can be sure of finding it: distinctions of the IS data when compared with the COULD BE but IS NOT data. This is the next step in Problem Analysis.

What changes are most likely to suggest the cause of our problem? Those that are most relevant to its peculiar features of identity, location, timing, and magnitude. Suppose there had been eight operational and/or maintenance changes in the filter house over the past six months. Even if we knew the exact number and kind of changes that had occurred, which ones would we want to examine first? Six changes that affected all five filters? Or two that affected only Number One? Seven that affected operations during the past six months? Or one that was instituted only a day or a week before the problem was first observed?

When we ask of each distinction, "Does this distinction suggest a change?" we are going straight for the changes capable of suggesting cause. We are bypassing any changes that *may have occurred but that are not relevant* to the key features of this problem. The relationship of distinctions and changes, and the relationship of both to the generation of possible causes, are very important.

Suppose, when the problem was first recognized, that a problem analyst had been presented with the distinction of the square-cornered gasket on the leaking filter. He or she might not have grasped its significance. Why not? Because unimportant distinctions abound between one thing and another and between one period of time and another. Compare any two pieces of equipment that have been in place for a few years and you will usually find a number of distinctive features about each. Parts have broken and been repaired. New, perhaps slightly different parts have replaced worn-out ones. Operating procedures may vary slightly from one to the other for any of a dozen reasons.

The leaking filter might have had a different type of gasket for five years yet never leaked until recently. *But when this distinction is appreciated as representing a change*—and a change that occurred the evening before the leaking was observed—*its significance as a clue is greatly heightened.*

To the distinctions of the IS data as compared with the IS NOT data, we now add the change question and the answers to it. This is shown in Figure 5, shown on page 51.

Generation of Possible Causes

Somewhere in the lists of distinctions and changes that emerge during Problem Analysis lies the explanation of cause—provided that all relevant information about the problem has been obtained and included. Several possible causes sometimes will emerge. Pieces of information must be knitted together in some cases to provide a satisfactory explanation of the problem's cause. Two changes operating in combination may produce a performance deviation that one of those changes alone cannot.

The way to generate possible causes is to ask of each item in the categories of distinction and change, "How could *this*

Figure 4.   **Deviation Statement:**

	SPECIFYING QUESTIONS	PERFORMANCE DEVIATION
IDENTITY	WHAT is the unit with the malfunction?	IS Number 1 Filter
	WHAT is the malfunction?	IS leaking oil
LOCATION	WHERE is the malfunction observed (geographically)?	IS observed at northeast corner of filter house
	WHERE on the unit is the malfunction observed?	IS observed at the cleanout hatch
TIMING	WHEN was the malfunction first observed?	IS first observed three days ago
	WHEN has it been observed since?	IS observed continually, all shifts
	WHEN in the operating cycle of the unit is the malfunction first observed?	IS first observed as soon as oil goes into filter at start of shift
MAGNITUDE	WHAT is the EXTENT of the malfunction?	IS 5–10 gallons of oil leaked per shift
	HOW MANY units are affected?	IS Number 1 Filter only
	HOW MUCH of any one unit is affected?	N/A

Number One Filter Leaking Oil

CLOSEST LOGICAL COMPARISON	WHAT IS DISTINCTIVE ABOUT . . .
COULD BE but IS NOT Numbers 2–5	Number 1 Filter, when compared with Numbers 2–5? *Number 1 has a square-cornered gasket; the other four have rounded gaskets.*
(No logical comparison)	
COULD BE but IS NOT observed at other filter locations	The northeast corner of the filter house when compared with other filter locations? *This location is nearest to feedwater pump, exposing Number 1 Filter to higher level of vibration than affects other four filters.*
COULD BE but IS NOT observed at valves, pipes, locking mechanism	The cleanout hatch when compared with valves, pipes, locking mechanism? *The cleanout hatch is opened and refastened daily at every shift.*
COULD BE but IS NOT observed before three days ago	Three days ago, at start of shift, when compared with the period of time before that? *There was a monthly maintenance check just prior to start of shift three days ago.*
COULD BE but IS NOT observed when unit is not in use	Continual leaking, all shifts, when compared with not leaking when the unit is not in use? *Oil flows through the unit under pressure only when filter is in use.*
COULD BE but IS NOT first observed at a time later on in shift	Start of shift when compared with any time later on during shift? *First time oil comes into filter under pressure.*
COULD BE but IS NOT less than 5, more than 10 gallons per shift	5–10 gallons of oil leaked per shift when compared with less than 5 or more than 10?
COULD BE but IS NOT Filters 2–5	(No information not already noted above)
N/A	N/A

distinction (or *this* change) have produced the deviation as described in the deviation statement?" Just as pieces of information may have to be knitted together, they may just as often fall together, as happens in this case. Beginning at the top of our chart—distinctions and changes relative to *Identity*—we immediately notice the combination of a distinction and change:

> *Possible Cause:* Square-cornered gasket (distinction between Number One Filter and the other four) from the new supplier (change represented in that distinction) is too thin and of uneven construction. This caused the Number One Filter to leak oil.

Other possible causes can be generated from the distinctions and changes in our analysis. They will not appear to be strong contenders (because they are not and because you already know the explanation) but they are possible. We will describe them in order to help explain the testing step of Problem Analysis in the following section.

One possible cause can be derived from the dimension of Location. It was noted that the northeast corner of the filter house, where Number One stands, contains the feedwater pump. This distinction has some significance: the leaking filter is exposed to considerably greater vibration than the other four filters. This represents no change. It has always been that way. We know from the specification, moreover, that the present leaking is occurring at the cleanout hatch, not at the valves. When vibration had caused leakage in the past, it had occurred at the valves. Nevertheless, at this point in Problem Analysis we should generate all reasonable possible causes, not select the problem's true cause. Vibration is given the benefit of the doubt.

> *Possible Cause:* Vibration from feedwater pump in northeast corner of filter house (distinction in the dimension of location) causes Number One Filter to leak oil.

4. Testing for Most Probable Cause

The last statement is listed as a possible cause simply because it is possible. That's important. By including *all* possible causes we lose nothing, maintain our objectivity, and reduce the incidence of conflict and disagreement in the explanation of a problem. In the testing step of Problem Analysis, we let the facts in the specification perform the function of judging the relative likelihood of possible causes.

Figure 5. **Deviation Statement: Number One Filter Leaking Oil**

	WHAT IS DISTINCTIVE ABOUT . . .	DOES THE DISTINCTION SUGGEST A CHANGE?
IDENTITY	Number 1 Filter, when compared with Numbers 2 through 5? *Number 1 has a square-cornered gasket; the other four have rounded gaskets.*	Square-cornered gasket is a new type, installed for first time three days ago at monthly maintenance check.
LOCATION	The northeast corner of the filter house when compared with other filter locations? *This location is nearest to feedwater pump, exposing Number 1 Filter to higher level of vibration than affects other four filters.*	Nothing. Location and level of vibration have been the same for years.
	The cleanout hatch when compared with valves, pipes, locking mechanism? *The cleanout hatch is opened and refastened daily at every shift.*	Nothing. Filter has been cleaned, hatch refastened on every shift for years.
TIMING	Three days ago, at start of shift, when compared with the period of time before that? *There was a monthly maintenance check just prior to start of shift three days ago.*	New type, square-cornered gasket installed for first time three days ago (as noted above).
	Continual leaking, all shifts, when compared with not leaking when the unit is not in use? *Oil flows through the unit under pressure only when filter is in use.*	Nothing
	Start of shift when compared with any time later on during shift? *First time oil comes into filter under pressure.*	Nothing
MAGNITUDE	5–10 gallons of oil leaked per shift when compared with less than 5 or more than 10?	
	(No information not already noted above)	N/A

We ask of each possible cause, "*If* this is the true cause of the problem, then how does it explain each dimension in the specification?" The true cause *must* explain each and every aspect of the deviation, since the true cause created the *exact* effect we have specified. Effects are specific, not general. Testing for cause is a process of matching the details of a postulated cause with the details of an observed effect to see whether that cause could have produced that effect. For example:

If vibration from the feedwater pump is the true cause of Number One Filter leaking oil, *then* how does it explain *why:*

LOCATION: Leaking IS observed at the cleanout hatch; IS NOT observed at the valves, pipes, or locking mechanism.

TIMING: Leaking IS observed three days ago; IS NOT observed before three days ago.

Vibration previously affected the valves and *not* the cleanout hatch. It doesn't make sense to say that vibration causes a cleanout hatch to leak. Why would vibration cause leaking to begin three days ago and not before? Unless we are willing to make some rather broad assumptions, we cannot make this possible cause fit the observed effects. Our judgment tells us that this is a sloppy explanation at best.

Another possible cause is suggested by the distinctions and changes found in our analysis:

Possible Cause: New maintenance people (a distinction that also represents a change in the dimension of timing) are not closing the cleanout hatch properly, possibly not using a torque wrench. This is causing Number One Filter to leak.

Testing this possible cause with our "If. . .then. . ." question, we quickly find ourselves at a loss to explain why leaking should appear only on Number One and not on the other four filters. After all, the same people are responsible for maintaining all five filters. If they failed to tighten Number One properly, why would they do a good job on all the others? We would have to make broad assumptions to make the cause fit the observed effects: "Well, they probably use the torque wrench on the other four. But back in the northeast corner of the filter house, where it's so dark and there's all that vibration from the feedwater pump, they figure the hell with it and don't tighten the cleanout hatch the way they should." This is an even sloppier explanation than the other one.

The actual cause fits all the details of the effect as specified: a new, thinner, square-cornered gasket that was put on Number One three days ago during the monthly maintenance check. It explains the *Identity* of the malfunction, its *Location*, *Timing,* and *Extent.* It requires no assumptions at all to make it work. It fits as hand does to glove, as cause and effect *must* fit. The relative likelihood of each of the other possible causes is small.

Testing a possible cause against the specification is an exercise in logic. It identifies the most likely possible cause that explains the deviation *better* than any of the other possible causes—but it seldom proves the true cause beyond the shadow of a doubt.

5. *Verification of the True Cause*

To *verify* a likely cause is to *prove* that it did produce the observed effect. In our example all we need to do is obtain a gasket with rounded corners from the old supplier, install it, and see if the leaking stops. Or we can trade the gasket from Number One for the non-leaking gasket from one of the other filters. Either action would prove that the leaking resulted from installation of a new, thinner gasket bought at a bargain price.

Verification is easy to perform once you have identified a likely cause. It consists of asking an additional question or two or setting up an experiment (such as trading the gaskets). It depends on bringing in *additional information* and taking an *additional action.* Verification is an independent step taken to prove a cause-and-effect relationship.

Sometimes no verification is possible and we must rely on the testing step alone: A rocket booster explodes in flight. Most of the tangible evidence is destroyed. We would certainly not want a second such accident. All that can be done—based on the paperwork of Problem Analysis up through testing of possible causes against the specification—is to devise corrective action based on the most probable cause. Assumptions are unavoidable. "If *this* happened, then *that* would make sense. . . ."

Verification is possible in most problem situations. What it consists of will depend on the circumstances. A mechanical problem may be duplicated by consciously applying a distinction or change that seems highly indicative of cause. Many problems are verified by "putting on the old gasket"—that is, reversing a change to see whether the problem stops. In that case verification provides corrective action. Resolution coincides with the last step in the process of Problem Analysis.

Failure

Of course we may fail. While the most common cause of failure is too little data in the specification, there are two major reasons for failing to solve a problem despite use of Problem Analysis:

1. Insufficient identification of key distinctions and changes related to the IS data in the specification.

2. Allowing assumptions to distort judgment during the testing step. The greater the number of assumptions we tack onto a possible cause in order to label it "most probable," the less chance there is that it will survive verification. There is nothing wrong with making assumptions as long as we regard them as such and not prematurely grant them the status of fact.

A Process, Not a Panacea

Thousands of people have used these techniques to solve problems that seemed otherwise unsolvable or solvable only by far greater expenditure of time and money. Most of the same people have failed to solve other problems they were sure they could crack—"if only they had stayed with the process." Problem Analysis enables us to do a good job of gathering and evaluating information about problems. However, there are limitations to the power of the process to produce the right answers. If we cannot track down the key facts needed to crack a problem, that problem will continue to defy solution. No approach or process, however systematically or meticulously applied, will unlock its secret.

Chapter Summary

The shadows cast by our problems may be perplexing. Yet the *structure* of *all* problems is always the same. It is knowledge of this structure that enables us to move systematically from definition to description to evaluation to hypothesis to verification of cause.

- The **Deviation Statement** is our concise description of both the object of our concern and the defect or malfunction for which we want to find the cause. In our example that statement was "Number One Filter Leaking Oil."

- The **Specification** of the problem is a comprehensive description of the problem's identity, location, timing, and magnitude—as it IS and as it COULD BE but IS NOT. The Number One Filter IS leaking; each of the other four COULD BE but IS NOT. The location of the leaking IS the cleanout hatch; leaking COULD BE but IS NOT observed at the valves, pipes, or locking mechanism. From the identification of this IS. . .COULD BE but IS NOT data, we assemble bases of comparison that will lead us to an understanding and resolution of the problem.

- We look for **Distinctions**—features that characterize only the IS data in all four dimensions. We ask, "What is *distinctive* about the Number One Filter *when compared with* Filters Two through Five?" We carry this kind of questioning through the other three dimensions. The result is a collection of key features that characterize the identity, timing, location, and magnitude of our problem.

- We then study each distinction to determine whether it also represents a **Change.** It is at this point in our analysis that we recognize the square-cornered gasket on the leaking filter—not only as a distinctive feature of that filter *but as a change*. Until the day before the problem appeared, Number One Filter had been equipped with the same type of round-cornered gasket used on the other units.

- When all distinctions and changes have been identified, we begin to **Generate Possible Causes.** Each distinction and change is examined for clues to cause. Each resultant hypothesis of cause is stated to illustrate not only what caused the problem but how it did so: "Square-cornered gasket from new supplier is too thin and of uneven construction. This caused Number One Filter to leak."

- Each possible cause we generate is then **Tested** against the specification. It must explain both the IS and IS NOT data in each dimension. In order to graduate to the status of MOST PROBABLE CAUSE, it must explain or withstand all the facts in the specification. Unless we make some far-fetched assumptions, "greater vibration in the northeast corner of the filter house," for example, cannot explain either the leak at the location on the filter or the time period that characterized this problem. Vibration, as a possible cause, is less likely to have produced the problem than the installation of the new gasket.

- The final step in Problem Analysis is **Verification** of the most probable cause. Unlike the testing step, which is a paper test, the verification is carried out in the work environment if possible. In our example and in most problem situations, this can be done in two ways: either by duplicating the effect according to the suggestions of cause in the analysis, or by reversing the change suspected of having caused the problem to see if the problem stops.

If no possible cause that has been generated passes the testing step, or if no cause that does pass it survives the step of verification, the only recourse is to tighten up the prior work. We may need more detailed information in the specification, in the ensuing identification of distinctions of the IS data, and in the identification of changes represented in the distinctions. This may lead to new insights, to the generation of new possible causes, and finally to a successful resolution.

Failure to find the true cause of a problem through these techniques is a failure in either the gathering or the use of information. You cannot use information that you do not have. If you get the information but use it carelessly, the result may be no better.

The logic of Problem Analysis defends conclusions that support facts; it sets aside those that cannot. It is a process that makes use of every bit of experience and judgment we possess. It helps us to use both in the most systematic and objective way possible.

Problem Analysis enables people to work together as a team, pooling their information in a common format to determine the cause of a problem. Most deviations are so complex that one person alone does not have the information necessary to find, test, and verify the explanation. When all those who hold important data have a mechanism for integrating it, they can begin to find the unknown cause. Otherwise, that discovery may be stalled by misunderstandings and other barriers to communication.

CHAPTER 3

The Uses of Problem Analysis

Introduction:
Acquiring the Habit of Problem Solving

This chapter presents ways in which organizations have solved problems through improved use of cause-and-effect thinking.

Late in 1977 we asked General Carl Schneider, commander of a large United States Air Force base, about the *kinds* of results he had expected of the Kepner-Tregoe program that two years before had been installed throughout his command.

"The day I assumed this command," he said, "people were lined up outside my door. 'We thought we ought to see you before we do anything on this' was a typical opening line. In short they were asking me to take responsibility for their actions—not, I believe, because they really wanted me to but because they thought they had to operate that way. I had to convince them that they did not have to and that I didn't want them to. But you cannot just tell people, 'Look, you've got to solve your own problems!' You must provide them with both the skills and the confidence to do that.

"That was why we installed the Kepner-Tregoe program as a core feature of our overall organization development effort. With that we were able to say, 'Now, you've been given problem solving techniques that have been very successful for a great many people. We expect you to use them. The time to go to your superior is when you think you have the solution to a problem, when you're ready to present your case.' "

Throughout what General Schneider referred to as his "homemade organization development program" there was great emphasis on giving and taking responsibility. He believed this attitude would lead to a healthier and more productive organization. His tenure as Commanding Officer proved him right.

> He related an incident that had occurred about a month before our meeting. One Saturday (a non-working day for top level technical people) he had stopped in at the base to find some sixty of his staff carrying out a multi-faceted Problem Analysis. They were trying to determine the cause of cracks in the walls of F-111 aircraft engines.
>
> "Nobody had told me a thing about it. I had no idea the group had decided to spend their Saturday working on the problem. It was their decision as a team." Several days later the group presented General Schneider with their analysis of the problem. He asked a number of questions, approved their recommendations, and forwarded the analysis to the Pentagon with the strong suggestion that it be accepted and the proposed course of action adopted as soon as possible. As a direct result of that suggestion, the Pentagon one week later ordered nearly $9 billion worth of aircraft grounded for detailed inspection and repairs.

Most applications of Problem Analysis result, to be sure, in less dramatic conclusions. But the conditions that produced these particular conclusions were typical of conditions that have always produced the best results: The people who carried out the analysis had been given systematic problem-solving techniques. They knew how to apply them to the real problems on their jobs. They were rewarded for making the effort. They were not afraid of failure. To one degree or other, these conditions for habitual and successful problem solving are evident in all the examples that follow.

The preceding chapter laid the groundwork for full understanding of these examples of Problem Analysis in action. Each example touches on four general subjects:

- Problem Analysis questioning at the managerial level

- Abbreviated use of the process

- Resolution of situations in which a performance ACTUAL has never achieved the designated SHOULD

- Use of the techniques in a team situation

Problem Analysis Questioning at the Upper Managerial Level

Full step-by-step application of the process, documented on chartpad or notepad, is required most often for concrete problems whose identity can be directly observed or easily visualized. These largely are mechanical, tangible situations.

At the upper management level, however, application of the process often consists of use of the *ideas* of the process. This includes discussion of a situation in all its dimensions rather than formulation of hypotheses based on experience; attention to distinctions of identity, location, timing, and magnitude rather than informed speculation alone; and testing of possible causes against the facts surrounding a situation rather than immediate action directed at the cause suggested by informed speculation. Data may be recorded and notes taken, but use of the process at upper levels of management is usually observable in the character of the questioning and the nature of the investigation. We observe people using the common language of Problem Analysis to organize their information, communicate it, and put it in perspective. They are sharing information through the channels of a systematic process. They are using words that will clarify each individual's contributions.

Busy managers are not avoiding responsibility when they tell subordinates, "I want you to solve your own problems." They have neither the time nor the specific skills to personally guide their subordinates' problem-solving efforts. The truth of the matter is that managers who become directly involved in problem solving are subject to criticism for failing to set priorities on their own time or to delegate appropriately—in short, for failing to *manage* their operations. Managers need not have all the right answers. What *is* required of them are the ability and willingness to ask the right questions. The kind of questioning we use in specifying, in identifying distinctions and changes, and in testing possible causes lends itself well to the process of assessing the logic and the work that other people have contributed to resolving a problem.

Problem: The Bank in Hawthorne

One kind of problem that taxes our ability to ask the right questions is the problem that drifts in like fog, very gradually, until visibility has dropped to near zero. Some gradual change in conditions has occurred, and by the time the situation has become serious enough to gain everyone's attention its critical elements may be lost to view.

A major bank in California has a number of branches in the Los Angeles area. The operating results of all branches are reviewed monthly by the Executive Committee. At a July review, the Hawthorne branch showed a volume of transactions slightly below plan. All the other branches were right on target or above.

In August the Hawthorne branch slipped a little further, in September even more. In October the news was worse yet. Members of the Executive Committee began an investigation. One vice president suggested exploration of the subject of *change,* saying he had already given it some thought and pointing out that when the decline in transactions was observed the new branch manager had been in his position for about two months. "Look, he represents a change all right. He came in just before the branch started to slip. I thought we were making a mistake then and I'm sure of it now."

The committee went on to consider who might take over that position if the bank let the new manager go. After long discussion the chairman suggested that they might be jumping to cause on the basis of a single fact. He wanted the Committee to consider the decline in terms of an informal specification—to discuss the Identity, Location, Timing, and Magnitude of the decline. He wasn't taking anything away from the vice president's assessment. He just wanted to make sure the situation was investigated thoroughly and objectively before action was taken that would seriously affect the branch manager's career.

Despite some disagreement they began an objective analysis. In the dimension of Location, the Committee named the Hawthorne branch as the IS. It was in Hawthorne alone that the decline was observed. All other branches represented the IS NOT. The question "What is distinctive about the Hawthorne branch when compared with all other branches?" led to discussion of its proximity to International Airport and the factories of North American Aviation and Douglas Aircraft.

"Wait a minute," someone said. "North American has been stretching out work on the B-70 bomber and laying off people for some time. And Douglas is transferring a lot of its work from Hawthorne to Long Beach. . . ."

After discussing the gradual local economic decline that had resulted from these actions, the Committee concluded that the new manager deserved the benefit of the doubt. Because the economic situation in the Hawthorne area was not characterized by sudden, sharp, immediately identifiable change, the Committee had found it easier to seize on the new manager's performance as a likely cause of decreasing transactions. His appointment, after all, had been a more visible and recent change. Attention subsequently was focused on the new line of reasoning, supported by the efforts of at least one committee member to consider this answer to the problem.

Summary

By insisting on asking and answering questions in all dimensions of the problem situation—including but not confined to the new manager's performance—the chairman played a vital role in the process. He made it possible for the discipline of Problem Analysis to absorb responsibility for producing a reasonable possible cause for the decline, one that could respond to *all* the facts surrounding it. There was no loss of face nor was anyone blamed or fired for a situation that in no way could be termed mismanagement.

It was simple to check the theory of local economic decline as the true cause of the problem:

- When did volume first begin to fall off at Hawthorne? Early in July.

- When did layoffs begin at North American? In late May and early June.

- How long after a round of layoffs would the impact be felt in the bank? No more than two or three weeks.

- How would the impact show up initially? By a reduction in deposits, then an increase in withdrawals.

Verification consisted of a few hours of telephone research to check out the experience of other banks nearby. The same story was told by all.

Proper Uses of the Techniques

To make the techniques of Problem Analysis pay off on a day-to-day basis, there must be a commitment to use them properly. There must be willingness to ask *all* the questions needed to define a problem situation fully and to allow the facts surrounding that situation to speak for it. Speculations are useful only to the extent that they are made within the structure of the process. On the other hand, speculation that overrides the structure or that is couched in the language but not the spirit of the process can be devastating: note that the vice president suggested "exploration of the subject of *change*. . . ." His suggestion that the new branch manager was at fault was presented to the group on the basis of what has aptly been labeled a "process trinket."

Listen to the manager who coined this term: "People occasionally come to me with some idea they want to push through, and they've covered the whole thing with these 'process trinkets.' If it *looks* like Problem Analysis, if it *sounds* like it, then the idea will have a better chance of acceptance."

It is quite possible to give the *appearance* of systematic analysis to a recommendation that represents a solitary, biased viewpoint. Yet whoever controls the questioning and assessment of that recommendation controls its *management*. As one of General Schneider's aides once told us, "The General expects you to come to a recommendation based on your own analysis. But you would not like to be in the position of defending it to him if it were not strictly on the up-and-up."

Problem: The Rejected Circuits

The simple question "Why?" is a poor substitute for the four-dimensional questioning we use in Problem Analysis. Yet, whenever something goes wrong, it is second nature to ask "Why?" and then review the flood of answers in hope that one of them will instantly suggest the problem's actual cause. The usual rationalization for the "Why?" approach is that people have been hired for their expertise and experience. If they can't come up with answers for problems that occur in the operation, those people don't belong in their jobs. Concrete results arising from the combination of systematic techniques and technical expertise are the only things that will convince a manager that *questions are as important as answers.*

An electronics manufacturing company is involved in the demanding task of producing miniaturized printed circuitry. One day, the production quality fell off sharply and the number of rejected circuits skyrocketed. "Why?" demanded the boss. "Why?" echoed his subordinates. "Temperature in the leaching bath is too high," said one technician. So temperatures were lowered.

A week later, when rejects climbed still higher, temperatures were raised, then lowered again, then systematically varied up and down for days. Rejects remained astronomical. "Cleanliness is not what it should be. That's what's causing the trouble," someone offered. So everything was scrubbed, polished, filtered, and wiped. The rejects dropped, then rose again. Acid concentration was the next idea. Same results. Water purity was checked out on Wednesday, Thursday, and Friday. The possibility of oil transferred from the operator's fingertips received full scrutiny on the following Monday and Tuesday. Rejects still were high.

They might have remained high had not one supervisor begun to ask systematic questions. "What is wrong with the rejected pieces?" This produced the information that the acid leaching step of the printed circuit pattern was occurring unevenly—as if some waterborne contaminant in the leaching solution was inhibiting the action.

"When does it occur?" A check of the records showed that rejects were at their highest on Monday mornings, lower on Monday afternoons, and gone by noon on Tuesday.

This cast a different light on everything. Now nobody was asking "Why?" about the cause of a general, ill-defined deviation. Instead they focused on *what was distinctive about Monday mornings* compared with the rest of the week. They focused on what might have been changed that bore a relationship to this timing. An immediate distinction was recognized: "Monday morning is the first work period following the non-work period of the weekend." And what changed on Monday morning? On each Monday, as soon as the tap was turned, water that had stood in the lines over the weekend came into the printed circuit leaching laboratories.

The water used in the process had to go through intensive purification, since purity standards of a few parts per billion are required. A quick search turned up the fact that some valves had been changed several months before. These valves used a silicone packing material. As water stood in the lines over the weekend, enough of this silicone packing material had begun to diffuse into the water and degrade the leaching process. The result? Many rejections on Monday morning, fewer in the afternoon, and none after Tuesday noon. By then the contaminated water had been purged from the system.

Summary

The company could have asked "Why?" indefinitely without ever finding the cause of this problem. Once the question "When?" had been asked and answered, the people involved could focus their technical expertise where it would do the most good.

Regardless of the content of a problem, the search for specific and accurate answers demands specific and precise questions.

The Abbreviated Use of Problem Analysis

The best use of Problem Analysis is the use that works best. There is no particular virtue attached to slavish adherence to every step in the entire process if a brief, informal use of the ideas can reveal the cause of the problem. In fact the longer people use Problem Analysis, the more adept they become at singling out fragments of the process that apply to the kinds of problems they face every day. When people begin asking questions like "Has anything changed in the timing of this operation lately?" or "What stage was this process at just before you noticed the trouble?" they have made the transition between an academic appreciation of Problem Analysis techniques and internalization of their practical role in daily problem solving.

Problem: The Troubles Aboard Apollo XIII

The vast majority of Problem Analyses never see pen and paper. This is especially true of the abbreviated application of the process. The seriousness of a problem does not necessarily determine the length or complexity of the analysis required to resolve it. Some extremely serious problems have been solved through abbreviated uses of the process. They were so data-poor that full use could not be undertaken. Fragments of the process had to be relied on and combined with educated speculation to arrive at a most likely cause.

> Apollo XIII was on its way to the moon. Fifty-four hours and fifty-two minutes into the mission—205,000 miles from Earth—and all was well. Then John L. Swigert, Jr., duty commander at the

time, reported to Houston: "Hey, we've got a problem here. . . we've had a Main Buss B undervolt." This was an insider's way of saying that electrical voltage on the second of two power generating systems had fallen off and a warning light had appeared. A moment later the power came up again. Swigert reported: "The voltage is looking good. And we had a pretty large bang associated with the caution and warning there." Three minutes later, as the dimensions of the problem became more clear, he reported: "Yeah, we got a Main Buss A undervolt too. . . . It's reading about 25½. Main B is reading zip right now." Apollo XIII, carrying three people toward the moon at incredible speed, was rapidly losing power and could shortly become a dead body. A disaster had occurred in space and no one was sure what had happened.

On the ground at Houston, NASA engineers put Problem Analysis questioning to work immediately. They began to build a specification of the deviation from the information that came in answer to their questions and from data displayed on their monitoring equipment. At the same time they started a number of contingency actions to reduce use of electrical power in Apollo XIII. Thirteen minutes after the first report, Swigert reported: "Our O^2 Cryo Number Two Tank is reading zero. . .and it looks to me, looking out the hatch, that we are venting something. . . out into space. . .it's gas of some sort."

What had begun as an electrical problem—loss of voltage— became a sudden loss of oxygen in the second of two tanks, with a more gradual loss of oxygen from the first. Since oxygen was used in the generation of electricity as well as directly in life support systems, the situation could hardly be more serious.

Although no one could conceive at the time of what *might* have caused the tank to burst, "Rupture of the Number Two Cryogenic Oxygen Tank" *would* explain the sudden loss of voltage and the subsequent loss of pressure. Further actions were taken to conserve both oxygen and electricity. A number of "IS . . .COULD BE but IS NOT" questions were asked to get further data, and a series of system checks was undertaken to verify cause. In the end it was determined that the Number Two Tank had burst and vented all its oxygen plus a large portion of the gas from the Number One Tank through a damaged valve and out into space. The three men returned successfully to Earth but only by the narrowest of margins. Had the cause remained unknown for very much longer, they would not have had enough oxygen left to survive.

It was weeks before the root cause of this problem was established through on-the-ground testing and experimentation. Two weeks before the launch, a ground crew had piped liquid oxygen into the tanks in a countdown demonstration. After the test they had had difficulty getting the oxygen out of Number

Two Tank. They had activated a heater inside the tank to vaporize some of the liquid oxygen and so provide pressure to force it out. They had kept the heater on for eight hours, longer than it ever had been used before. Although a protective switch was provided to turn off the heater before it became too hot, the switch was fused in the ON position because the ground crew had connected it to a 65-volt power supply instead of the 28-volt supply used in Apollo XIII. Later, in flight, the crew turned the heater on briefly to get an accurate quantity reading. The fused switch created an arc that overheated the oxygen in the tank, raised the internal pressure tremendously, and blew the dome and much of the connecting piping off into space.

Summary

There was no time for NASA Houston to go through a complete listing of all the distinctions and changes they might observe. Instead they asked, "What *traumatic change* could cause the sudden, total failure in electrical generation?" A cutting-off of the flow of oxygen to the fuel cells would have that effect. They knew which fuel cells were inoperative when Swigert reported that Cryo Number Two Tank was reading zero. They tested cause—that Number Two Tank had ruptured—and found this would explain the suddenness and totality described in the specification. It also would account for the bang reported at the time of the first undervolt indication, a shuddering of Apollo XIII felt by flight crew members, and the venting of "something. . .out into space." It accounted both for the IS data they had amassed and IS NOT information that had come from their monitoring activities. But most important it explained a sudden, total failure within the system.

For the NASA Houston engineers, this cause was difficult to accept. They had unbounded faith in Apollo equipment, knowing that it was the best that could be devised. The idea of an oxygen tank bursting open in the depths of space? Not credible. All this was justified from their experience. Without the bungling that had occurred on the ground two weeks before the launch, the tank would have gone to the moon and back just as it was designed and built to do. However, the Houston engineers stuck to the Problem Analysis process despite their incredulousness, believing that the test for cause they had carried out had provided the correct answer. In fact they proved out this cause in record time. What saved the day was their knowledge of Apollo XIII systems and of what *could* produce the exact kind of sudden failure that had occurred.

In such a case Problem Analysis is rendered difficult by two factors: secondary effects and panic. Sudden failure in a complex system usually causes other deviations that may obscure the original deviation. The shock of a sudden failure often precipitates panic, making still more difficult a careful review and use of the facts. A disciplined and systematic investigation is difficult in any case, but discipline becomes essential when a top-speed search for cause is undertaken and there is no possibility of amassing all the data that would be optimal in the investigation. In the NASA incident, the presence of a systematic approach enabled a team of people to work together as a single unit even though they were separated from the deviation by nearly a quarter of a million miles.

Problem: The Spray Nozzles

The NASA example illustrates the chief motivation for use of an abbreviated version of Problem Analysis: lack of data and/or time needed to do a full-scale analysis. Another common motivator for short-cut Problem Analysis is expediency. It may simply be unnecessary to go into the full process in order to explain the deviation. Facts of Identity, Location, Timing, and Magnitude may suggest a reasonable, possible cause for the problem. If this possible cause can quickly be verified as true cause, all the better.

> A large city in California bought new spray equipment for painting white and yellow lines on roads. From the beginning the equipment gave the operators trouble even though no new procedures had been introduced. No critical change existed. The equipment was brand new. It was cleaned with solvent before being taken out on the job. After a short period of operation, the spray nozzles plugged up. The operators then stopped work, cleaned everything, and reassembled the equipment. Within minutes the nozzles plugged up again. It didn't take long for this problem to make a shambles of the work schedule of the Street and Transportation Department.
>
> A Problem Analysis was begun. The problem was specified. The only IS NOT available in terms of identity was the previously used paint sprayer. At that point, about two minutes into the analysis, someone said, "What if the solvent we are using is good for the old unit but not for the new one?" The manufacturer's instruction book turned up the fact that only ST-64 solvent must be

used on the new sprayer. "What solvent are we using?" "Same one we always used, Ajax Super-Kleen. It's the best one we can get." Best for what? Not the new paint sprayer. ST-64 was introduced and the new sprayer worked perfectly.

Summary

"Best for what?" applies equally well to the use of Problem Analysis. If a possible cause leaps to mind two minutes into the specification and can be verified easily and quickly as true cause, then that is the best use of the process for that situation. If a "Eureka" idea comes to mind in a minute and requires only minutes to verify, how much time is lost even if it fails?

Problem: Feeding the Cattle

Another abbreviation of Problem Analysis is useful in focusing on one apparently critical dimension in the specification. For example, distinctions and changes related to the timing of the problem may be studied intensively to the exclusion of everything else.

One of our clients produces cattle feed with soybean meal as an essential ingredient. Soybeans contain urease, an enzyme that reacts with urea to form ammonia. Urea is added to the meal to help the cattle convert it to protein. This means that the urease content must be controlled. If ammonia were produced, it could cause serious, even fatal, bloating in the cattle. So the meal is put through steam-heated toasters to control and reduce the urease. A laboratory analysis is run on urease levels each day.

For nine years there had been no trouble with urease levels in our client's plant. Carloads of cattle feed were produced every day. The lab analysis was run every day. Everything was as it should be. One day the routine laboratory test showed that the urease level was substantially above the standard. The results were reported immediately to the Plant Manager. After he embargoed all meal produced within the past forty-eight hours, he began to specify the problem in his mind. He quickly focused on the time dimension: "The urease level had been high all day today but appeared to have been normal right up through last night. Almost certainly something had changed today, this morning, and had lasted all day." For the present he would look only in this direction.

He went to the feed line and questioned the operators. What had they changed? What were they doing differently today? Nothing, as far as they knew. Everything was just the same as it had always been. Then he went to Engineering to find out about the equipment. "Anything changed today?" Nothing. He went to the lab to ask about the tests. Nothing. Then to Maintenance with the same question. "Oh, yeah. We had a new guy replacing a packing gland on the steam line." It turned out that the repairman had run into trouble and so had turned off the steam to one of the toasters all day. He didn't realize that the reduced temperature meant that the urease would be uncontrolled and the feed spoiled for cattle consumption.

A closer check by the lab showed eleven carloads affected. Other markets were found for the feed where the higher urease level would not be a problem. No customers suffered.

Summary

The Plant Manager understood that a change in some condition is what creates a deviation. He recognized that the change in this case probably had taken place during a very specific, recent period of time. If, after nine trouble-free years, serious trouble had developed this morning and continued all day, then change within the past twenty-four hours was the thing to track in all functions that could possibly account for an increase in urease levels.

Once the purpose of each of the steps in Problem Analysis is understood and a manager has internalized the rationale behind the progression of these steps, the steps can be pulled apart and applied to suit the particular needs of a situation. The structure of each problem is the same: deviation between actual and expected performance for which the cause is unknown. All the facts surrounding any problem fall into four dimensions: Identity, Location, Timing, and Magnitude. Comparative data in these four dimensions—the IS NOTS—provide the distinctions and changes that narrow the search for the cause of a problem. These and other basic tenets of Problem Analysis become second nature to people who use the process in part and in full on a daily basis. How much of it do you need to solve a problem? Just enough.

Conclusions

The Executive Committee chairman of the California bank knew that more was needed than a focus on one personnel change. The manager in the electronics company knew that

"Why?" must be supplanted by "What?" "Where?" "When?" "Extent?" before he could recognize the direction in which the analysis should go. Mission Control on Apollo XIII knew that the only choice it had was to do less than the full Problem Analysis it would have liked to do. Time and data were distressingly inadequate. The operators trying to figure out why a paint sprayer plugged up knew they had used enough of the process just two minutes after they began their analysis, when the explanation jumped out at them. The plant manager in the cattle feed manufacturing facility, given the nature of his problem, knew that an investigation of change in the dimension of timing was almost guaranteed to produce the right answers.

Examples of the successful use of abbreviated Problem Analysis all share one characteristic: They show that experience and judgment produce their best possible results when channeled through some or all of the elements of a systematic process.

Situations in Which Actual Performance Never Has Met Expectations

When we begin a Problem Analysis that concerns the "never has worked" kind of problem, it is sensible to examine the performance SHOULD itself and perhaps do a bit of research.

Is the SHOULD realistic? Has it ever been attained, anywhere by anyone? *Who* says it is the SHOULD? And based on what criteria? Sometimes performance standards are set carelessly or are purposely set at a higher level than anyone really expects to achieve. And sometimes a performance SHOULD is communicated in one way but meant in quite another.

Problem: The 8:30 Arrival

A vice president for sales and marketing, complaining about lack of drive in a recently hired salesman, was perplexed. The man had an excellent sales record with his previous employer.

We asked for an example of this lack of drive.

"OK, here's an example. I told him that when he's in town I expect him to be in the office by 8:30. At 8:30 on the dot, this guy walks through the door."

What is wrong with that?

"It irritates me that he walks in as the clock strikes. If nothing else, you'd think he'd show up before then to get his day organized. That's what I've always done. I guess I feel it's unprofessional behavior—like a kid slipping into his seat in class just as the bell rings."

Had any of this been communicated to the new employee?

"Of course not! It isn't the sort of thing you say."

Then how did the manager think the situation would ever resolve itself?

"I don't know. . . ."

About a month later we received a letter from the manager that included these remarks:

"I bit the bullet and talked to the man about coming in here at 8:30 sharp. He laughed. He said his wife was taking a class at a local college that started classes at 8:15 a.m. He dropped her off there and then came into the office, which is just about fifteen minutes from the college. If I preferred, he told me, she could drop *him* off at 8:00! The outcome of this somewhat embarrassing misunderstanding is that I have thought a lot about how I communicate with my staff. I looked at their jobs in terms of what you call SHOULD and I decided that I make too many assumptions. I don't tell people what I actually expect. Naturally they reciprocate by not doing it."

Summary

Human performance SHOULDS must be communicated clearly and fully. Equally important is a commitment on the part of the manager to make these SHOULDS reasonable. If they are not communicated clearly, or if they are unreasonable, then performance will be perceived as unacceptable even though the person is doing the best he or she can. This classic cause of misunderstanding between superior and subordinate has been experienced by nearly everyone from one side of such a misunderstanding or the other. It does not have to occur.

Problem: The Identical Unit

A deviation in degree is the most usual type of problem characterized by a Day One Deviation from SHOULD. Something performs fairly well, perhaps almost well enough—but never quite as well as it was supposed to. Instead of 100% achievement of a standard, we observe 92% or 95% efficiency day after day. This is a typical problem in a production plant, where 5% loss of efficiency on an important unit of equipment can result over time in substantial loss.

A chemical plant manufacturing a single product had one process unit that consistently produced at an acceptable level in quality and quantity. When demand for the product increased, management decided to purchase and install a second unit. This was done and the new, virtually identical unit went on line. From the beginning it underproduced. It was always from 5% to 7% less efficient than the original unit. Teams of technical people from the plant, the parent company, and the manufacturer worked the new unit over from top to bottom without discovering the cause.

The critical control on production yield depended on holding solids to a level of 15% at one point in the process. Samples were drawn from each of the units every hour and analyzed in the lab for solids content. Feeds, temperatures, and pressures were adjusted accordingly to maintain the 15% target. On the original unit the adjustment produced correct final yield. On the new unit (an exact duplicate of the original, according to the manufacturer) it did not. Final yields fluctuated regardless of adjustments.

After more than a year of investigation by experts, the plant manager authorized a team of five maintenance and repair personnel to have a go at the problem. All five had just been trained in Problem Analysis techniques. He felt they needed a miracle to come up with the cause of fluctuating yield on Number Two Process Unit.

The team made the initial assumption that the new unit could not be the identical twin of the original unit! Something within it or surrounding it must be different. Point by point, feature by feature, they made a comparative specification of the new unit (problem IS. . .) and the original one (problem COULD BE but IS NOT. . .). They set out to identify all distinctions relative to the identity, location, timing, and magnitude of the problem through examining the bases of comparison in their specification. After a great deal of work, only one substantial distinction could be found: Samples of product drawn from the new unit for laboratory solids analysis emerged at a point on the fractionating column just a bit higher than the draw-off point on the original unit. From this solitary distinction they postulated the following possible cause: "Samples drawn from Number Two Unit give a misleading solids level due to location of draw-off point." They could not explain *why* this should be so, but it was the best they could do.

"So what?" shrugged the technical people. "We knew that when the unit was installed. According to the manufacturer's design, there are a number of optional locations for that draw-off point. We used the one that was most convenient."

The team insisted that this difference in the draw-off location *might* lead to inaccurate readings and affect control over the process. Moreover, it would cost a grand total of $27 to move the sampling location on the new unit to match the location on the original unit. Experts were against it but the plant manager gave the go-ahead anyway. From the day the $27 was allocated, the 15% solids level on the new unit was achieved and maintained. The plant manager computed the value of lost production in the preceding year as something close to $700,000..

Summary

The *why* of the discrepancy of readings between one optional draw-off point and another could never be explained. There was a *critical distinction* between the units. There had to be. But even when found, this critical distinction was rejected by most people. It is worthy of note that a team of maintenance and repair personnel, without much technical expertise, was able to evaluate and solve this problem using simple, systematic techniques.

Conclusions

In many of our client companies, a Problem Analysis team always includes at least one member who has no technical expertise that bears directly on understanding the problem's *content*. This individual leads the process questioning. Time and again we have been told that inclusion of a non-expert has kept the team from getting bogged down in the details of the problem and giving undue weight to assumptions based on content expertise and technical background.

In a case in which performance has been acceptable up to a certain point in time, we know that we are looking for some kind of change in our search for cause. In a case in which performance has never been acceptable, we know that some *condition* necessary to achievement of the SHOULD does not exist now and never has existed. So we must focus on the *conditions of performance* and especially on *conditions that set apart the problem as it IS from all that it COULD BE but IS NOT* in terms of IDENTITY, LOCATION, TIMING, and MAGNITUDE. In other words, in the Day One Deviation, the search for cause must take place entirely in the area of distinctions.

Use of Problem Analysis Techniques by the Management Team

To one degree or another, all the examples that have appeared so far in this chapter reflect the shared use of Problem Analysis techniques. In this final section teamwork itself is our major focus: *how managers communicate and share information through the common language of the process to resolve problems they might not have been able to resolve individually.*

Problem: The Model A Sewing Machine

A very large merchandising house sells a private brand of sewing machines. The machines are manufactured for the house in six different models. For over a year the sewing machine line has not been selling as well as expected even though it was well received when it was first introduced. The Sales Promotion Manager, the Merchandising Manager, and the Sewing Machine Buyer finally met to analyze the problem. They began to specify the deviation, each contributing his or her special knowledge.

Their deviation statement was simple enough: "Sewing Machines Selling Poorly." They could not be more specific at the outset of the analysis, since the exact nature of the deviation—percentages of expected revenue achieved—was being explored in detail for the first time.

"What sewing machines?" was the first question, in the dimension of the problem's identity. They were prepared to say, "All six models." But when they began to review their data, they were startled to see that only Model A was selling poorly. Models B and C were selling somewhat better than A, and Models D, E, and F were selling quite well. None of the three managers had realized there were such marked differences in the rate of sales among the six models. Until then they had only been dealing with *average* figures. Almost immediately after beginning the specification, they went back to the deviation statement and revised it to read "Model A Sewing Machine Selling Poorly, Models B and C Selling Fairly Well. . . ." It did not look like a textbook deviation statement but it was more precise and useful than the first one.

They probed into the dimension of location and found that low sales of Model A were nationwide. There were no distinctions to be gleaned in terms of geographical factors such as "better in the Midwest, worst in the Northeast." Coast to coast, Model A sales were poor wherever Model A was available.

They hit paydirt when they turned their attention to the dimension of Timing. The records showed that the Model A machine had sold as well as expected in the first couple of months but then had fallen off sharply. Models B and C also had sold well and then had fallen off—but not as sharply as Model A. Models D, E, and F had sold well when first introduced and had continued to do so right up to the present time.

The discrepancies between the IS and IS NOT information were inescapable. They couldn't be ignored and they wouldn't go away. There was something distinctive about the Model A machine, and about the B and C models to a lesser degree, when compared with the models that were selling well.

The Merchandising Manager suggested an explanation: "Model A has fewer attachments and selling benefits. Perhaps it's simply a less desirable unit!" It was a neat explanation but unfortunately not so. "The fact is," said the Sewing Machine Buyer, "there isn't much difference among the attachments of the six units." She thought it made more sense to look at differences in sales features.

"That won't wash," said the Sales Promotion Manager. "Sales features for the six machines have been constant from the start. Anyway, how could that possibly account for a falloff on Model A beginning a couple of months *after* its introduction?"

The Merchandising Manager then brought up the subject of motivation. "Could there be some lack of motivation to *sell* Model A?" The Sales Promotion Manager replied, "The salesperson makes the lowest commission on Model A, the next lowest on Models B and C, and the best commission on the other three. That's normal enough—and besides, it doesn't represent any kind of change. It's always been that way."

After a few moments of silence, while everyone digested this information, the Sewing Machine Buyer asked, "Wouldn't there be some lapse of time *after* a new item is introduced before the salespeople begin to receive their commissions and figure which sales bring in the greatest return? I mean, maybe the realization that the commission rate on Model A is substantially lower than on Models D, E, and F would take a little time to sink in. After a couple of months their motivation to sell Model A might have changed."

The team decided that this explanation was the most likely cause of Model A's poor sales. To verify it the Sales Promotion Manager raised the commission rate on Model A, leaving price and all other variables the same. Within two months the Model A machine began to sell better.

Summary

In this meeting the three managers were able to contribute from their own areas of expertise. Equally important, each manager was able to question the others, within the structure of the process, to provoke ideas and expand the capability of the others to truly *analyze* the problem, not just talk about it. "*Could* this be a distinction?" one asked another. "*Does* that represent any change?" Each manager had unique inputs to make but all had the same understanding of the structure and progression of Problem Analysis. All were intent on the same goal: explaining the problem's cause. How different an approach it is from that in which each of three managers focuses on building a case to support a pet theory of cause.

Problem: The Irrigation Project

Sometimes a decision must be made about the way to correct a situation. Everyone agrees that *some* kind of corrective action is needed but there is not enough understanding of the situation's cause to enable the decision makers to say *what* kind of corrective action makes the most sense. This is the case in the following example, in which a Problem Analysis is required before the managers can move into the decision making process.

> A United States Government manager had a tough decision to make: what to do about an irrigation project the U.S. was financing in a Mideastern nation. Pumps that had been installed in wells some eighteen months earlier were now failing. The local employees didn't know how to maintain them and it was the manager's job to institute a training program. The Government had $20 million in the project and was prepared to spend half a million more on training.

> At first this manager didn't see the situation as one characterized by "cause unknown." To him the cause was obvious: the local employees didn't know how to maintain the pumps. Then, when one of his assistants began to ask some probing questions, he realized that he didn't know *for certain* what was causing poor maintenance.

> He called a meeting of his entire staff to specify the problem. He was shocked to find that the IS specification described the deterioration of *everything* having to do with the project: wells, weirs, pumps, ditches, shacks, tools—the whole works. The IS NOT was nothing more than "Not pumps alone. . . ." This knocked out the assumed cause, "Local Employees Don't Know How to Maintain Pumps." After all, how much technical expertise is required to maintain ditches, shacks, and weirs?

> He went on to ask, "Where is the deviation?" "IS in Country X; IS NOT in Countries Y and Z." (Y and Z were countries in which

a similar program was in effect. The level of technical expertise of local employees there was about the same as in X.) "When was the deviation first observed?" The IS specification, in Country X, was "from the inception of the program." The IS NOT, in Countries Y and Z, was there "had *never* been a difficulty with pump maintenance" even though the program in Country Y had been in effect nearly twice as long as in Country X.

"Extent?" In Country X "about 60% of the installations had deteriorated." The IS NOT was that "40% had not" and that "none had deteriorated in Countries Y and Z." The deviation had reached crisis proportions in Country X, threatening crop failure and famine.

Members of staff now began to ask what was *distinctive about Country X* compared with Countries Y and Z? And what was *distinctive about 60% of the installations* in Country X, where there was deterioration, compared with the 40% where there was none?

"Well, one thing, obviously," said an agronomist on the staff. "Land ownership patterns. There are many more tenant farmers in Country X than in Y and Z—small farmers working land they don't own."

"They are little more than serfs of the landlord owners," added an economist. "I would say that about 60% of the installations in Country X are maintained by tenant farmers."

The team manager asked the economist how many installations in Countries Y and Z would probably be maintained by tenant farmers. "Why, practically none. It's a totally different pattern of ownership in those countries."

Now the situation took on an entirely different light. The installations that were going to pieces were maintained by tenant-serfs with no stake in the success of the project. Installations that continued to function were maintained by farmer-owners. This had been the case from the inception of the project, so there was no change to cause the deviation. A condition of life had produced a predictable outcome. People with an incentive to maintain wells, weirs, pumps, and other equipment had somehow managed to stretch their mechanical skills to do the job. By contrast, laborers who received no benefit from the project, but only an additional burden, had let things go.

Summary

It is dangerous to assume the cause of a deviation when it has never been properly analyzed or verified. In this example the experts all thought they knew the cause: "The local employees can't maintain something as complicated as a pump." It made all kinds of sense—except that it didn't make any sense. Its inadequacy as an explanation didn't become apparent until the deviation was specified precisely and the inputs of staff members with different kinds of expertise were brought to bear on the development of distinctions.

A decision based on incorrect understanding of the situation's cause is of little or no help; it may actually make matters worse. If the manager involved in the irrigation project had recommended a series of costly maintenance training schools, scattered about the country (as he had been about to do), a great deal of time and at least half a million dollars would have been wasted. The deviation would have continued to exist and other equally useless actions would probably have been taken, further compounding the confusion. Only when the actual cause of the situation was known could an efficient incentive program be instituted—for it was motivation, not ability, that was the core of the problem.

Problem: Strikes and Issues

Before people have had actual experience with Problem Analysis in a team situation, they may sometimes imagine that the process is too rigid, that it deprives the team of spontaneity and creativity. They may visualize managers trudging a mental assembly line from deviation statements to verified causes. If that perception were true, Problem Analysis would indeed cramp anyone's style. Fortunately it is not so, as the following example makes clear.

> The top Industrial Relations people of an auto company are meeting to discuss an urgent labor problem. A confused issue about work rules has suddenly arisen in three stamping plants, and there is serious danger of a wildcat strike that will shut them all down. Shutting down the stamping plants will idle all the assembly lines within a few days, just when the peak sales period is rapidly approaching. The timing couldn't be worse. Union leaders from the three plants have made serious demands. Top management has given orders to the Industrial Relations people to avoid a strike if at all possible.
>
> "Why an issue like *this*, and why *now?*" asks the group's chairman, thinking about the dimensions of WHAT and WHEN. "It doesn't make sense to me." The situation is discussed at length. "All three plants are making these demands but the ones in Plant A are most strident," says another person, thinking of IS and IS NOT. "Why should Plant A be more interested in this than the

others?" asks someone else, looking for a distinction. "Aha! It's the only plant of the three with a possible jurisdictional conflict. They have two unions fighting for power in this particular trade." This statement by the chairman, who spotted the distinction, is followed by a discussion of the union squabbles.

"You know," says one man, drawing on his experience to suggest a possible cause, "it *could* be that there's a jurisdictional dispute going on underground at Plant A."

"That," someone else puts in, "is pure speculation."

"Look," says the first man, "*if* it were so, then someone may have worked up a possible wildcat strike to get added leverage for his own position. And if so, then I'll bet it doesn't have a thing to do with the issue itself. The other two plants would be going along just to give support to that faction. I know it's speculative but it fits the facts."

"And I know what you're thinking," says the man who had interrupted him. "If there's something like that going on, then Charlie Olson is mixed up in it."

"It isn't hard to guess what he would want," the chairman interjects, doing a little mental testing of the possible cause. "He's president of one union. If he wants to freeze out another union, this could do it. Nobody has more to gain in a jurisdictional fight than Olson." To verify cause through the additional data, they make a phone call to the IR Director at Plant A. Sure enough, word comes back that Olson is deeply involved.

Based on extended speculations within the basic thinking pattern of Problem Analysis and confirmed by the involvement of a key person, the IR people conclude that this is a jurisdictional matter. The dispute has nothing to do with work rules. They then develop a new approach: The company makes a quiet intervention at Plant A, the jurisdictional question is set to one side, and talk of a strike disappears overnight. A verbal Problem Analysis has come to its successful completion.

Summary

What these managers did was *speculate on facts of Identity and Location* that, if true, *would* explain the situation. Then they checked them out. If their speculations had proven incorrect, nothing would have been lost. As they turned out to be totally correct, the managers gained a great deal by being willing to make speculations based on experience and being willing to accept whatever facts would develop based on further investigation of the situation. Had they not speculated, they might not have found the cause of the threatened strike in time. Had they not checked out Olson's involvement to be sure that it was a factor, their problems might have increased ten-fold as they looked for a red herring until the last moment, only to discover that the real cause lay ̣elsewhere.

Problem: The NASA Suit

In our final example of how Problem Analysis is used by a management team, a serious and costly problem is analyzed not by one team but by several teams in two organizations.

> An electronics company obtained a NASA contract to produce a complicated item originally designed by a prestigious research laboratory. The equipment was completed, delivered, and installed but failed to work.
>
> NASA sued the company to recover $880,000 in payments already made. The plant manager argued that his company had manufactured the equipment exactly according to the specifications given by NASA. NASA's position was that the equipment didn't work, so NASA should not and would not pay for it. At the electronics company, the plant manager's head office was on his back for botching the job.
>
> Looked at in one way, it was NASA's problem. But the responsibility for discovering the cause of the deviation in performance—total failure of operation—lay not with NASA but with the top technical group in the company that had produced the equipment. Several teams began breaking down the specifications for this equipment into individual requirements in order to get total visibility of the basic elements of its design. They then compared the test and performance data they had generated against the specifications to see if their translation of the design into hardware had been at fault. They concluded that they had followed the design to the letter and that there was nothing wrong in what they had done. Now that the specifications had been broken down and laid bare, however, it became painfully evident that *the design itself was faulty.* One element of the design ignored a basic law of physics! In short, they had meticulously produced something that could not work. The plant manager took this analysis to NASA and convinced Agency officials that his people had done their work correctly—but that no one could produce equipment that would work from such a design.

The suit was withdrawn and NASA turned its attention to the research lab that had produced the faulty design. Thus, the lab was presented not with a *problem,* in our terminology—for cause was now known—but with a *decision,* a requirement for some kind of action. More importantly, the lab faced the need to develop procedures to prevent similar disasters in the future.

Chapter Summary

Problem Analysis was not developed with improved communication in mind. It was developed as a system that would make best use of a manager's natural cause-and-effect thinking pattern. Yet, over the years, the process has gained an impressive reputation as a communications device by virtue of its common language for problem solving and because it can be used by a team of people whose technical backgrounds, experiences, and outlooks are dissimilar. Managers continue to use the basic ideas of Problem Analysis in team situations because the ideas pay off time and again.

In order to get the maximum contribution of relevant information from a number of people working on one problem, some kind of structure is essential. It is also essential that people understand each other's words. You have probably seen this little sign on an office wall or desk: "I know that you believe you understand what you think I said, but I am not sure you realize that what you heard is not what I meant!" It may be the truth, sometimes, but it isn't the SHOULD. . . .

Problem Analysis techniques help people work together in organizing information so that cause-and-effect relationships can clearly be seen. The techniques provide both a way of testing cause and a framework of information to use in further verifying cause. The techniques provide a procedure for cutting into any deviation, regardless of its content, to arrive at mutual understanding of its components. Finally, by providing effective conditions for investigation, the techniques give assurance and confidence to those making the analysis along with a common orientation that reduces confusion, minimizes arguments, and encourages teamwork.

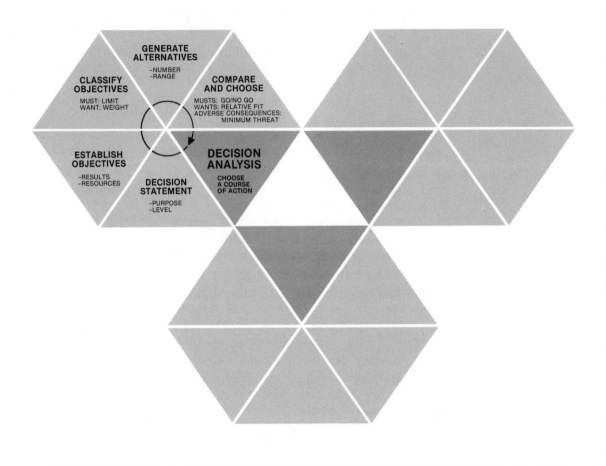

CHAPTER 4

Decision Analysis

Introduction:
The Conditions and Elements of Making Choices

Decisions must be made in all organizations and actions must be taken. It is up to the appropriate people in the organization to select the actions, determine how to carry them out, and take responsibility for their successful implementation. But there is often confusion over decisions. People find it hard to think together about the choices they must make. They don't agree on where to start or how to proceed. As a result they may overlook important information, fail to consult the proper people, and make mistakes. Organizational decision making is often not as good as it should be.

People enjoy being involved in decision making. In an organization, however, many shun the task because of the controversy involved. Lacking commonly accepted, unbiased procedures, decision making becomes a shoving contest among those with differing points of view. The individuals with the most power prevail. Others accept decisions in order to save face and avoid direct confrontation.

When people are provided with a common approach to decision making, they find they can indeed work as a team. There is more sharing of relevant information. Differing positions are more successfully reconciled because the process of decision making is less biased. Inevitably, the quality of decision making improves.

The Thinking Pattern for Making Choices

Decision Analysis is a systematic procedure based on the thinking pattern we all use in making choices. Its techniques represent expansions and refinements of the elements in this thinking pattern:

- We appreciate the fact that a choice must be made.

- We consider the specific factors that must be satisfied if the choice is to succeed.

- We decide what kind of action will best satisfy these factors.

- We consider what risks may be attached to our final choice of action that could jeopardize its safety and success.

We may employ this thinking pattern very swiftly, even unconsciously. Although we may skip one or more of its elements in a cursory analysis, each element plays some role in determining every choice we make. When we are confronted with simple, repetitive choices, memory and experience enable us to consider in a fraction of a second the specific factors that must be satisfied. This is seen typically in the choices we make when we drive an automobile. We would be incapable of driving without this ability to use automatically all the elements of the choice-making thinking pattern.

Nobody needs to be told that excellence in making choices is critical to individual and organizational success. Everyone knows that choices made today influence our lives tomorrow. What is not so obvious is *how* to make the decision today, using available information, that will be lauded as excellent tomorrow and bring credit to everyone associated with it. Nor is it so obvious *how* we ought to use that information, how we can avoid getting bogged down in details, how we can avoid missing the details that must be recognized, and how we can escape being confused and intimidated by the uncertainties of the future.

Behind most decisions lie myriad details. Some are highly important, some insignificant. The quality of available information may not match our needs. There may not be enough information. There may be so much that it overwhelms us. Perhaps the degree of relevance of available information is unclear. Over every decision hovers some measure of uncertainty—for all decisions will play out their day on a stage somewhere in the uncertain future. Good decision making, like good problem solving, depends heavily on experience and judgment. In both areas of managerial responsibility, however, it is within the framework of a *systematic procedure* that experience and judgment produce successful results and a reputation for managerial excellence.

The Elements of a Good Choice

Making good choices depends on three elements: the quality of our *definition* of specific factors that must be satisfied, the quality of our *evaluation* of the available alternatives, and the quality of our *understanding* of what those alternatives can produce—for better or worse. It all sounds so straightforward that we wonder how bad decisions come to be made. Here is one simple and highly typical example.

> "We need to increase the research and development capabilities of this organization." That was the statement made by a member of the Executive Committee of a fast-growing social research organization.
>
> Over a period of two months, the Committee discussed this need and considered alternative actions. With what result? The Committee hired a new Director of R&D, an individual who had worked for a competitor and was considered "the best."
>
> "Best for *what?*" is the question that should have been asked when the statement of need was first made.
>
> After the new Director had been in the job for six months, the Executive Committee came to three conclusions: (1) The new Director was not "best" for their organization. (2) The alternative of "new Director" did not really address any of the firm's pressing R&D concerns. (3) The question of a suitable direction for R&D at that point in the company's life had never been adequately discussed.
>
> The Committee had made a poor decision. Why? Because it had no clear purpose and had not discussed the organization's specific needs in matters of research and development. Consequently, the Committee had not understood the kinds of alternatives most likely to benefit the organization. Yet at the time the decision was made everyone was positive and enthusiastic about the choice.
>
> "What we said later," one member of the Committee told us, "was that given the information we had at the time it seemed like the right way to go. But I don't buy it. Given the information we *could* have had and the actions we *might* have taken had we really thought through our situation, I don't believe that the decision to hire 'the best' away from a competitor would have seemed

like the right way to go. Everyone was hung up on the assumption that there was somebody out there who could come in and work miracles. It was never put in just those words, but it was on that assumption that the whole decision was really based."

Many, many decisions are characterized by this kind of thinking. A good decision can only be made in the context of *what it is that needs to be accomplished.* No alternative is any better than its ability to do the job that has to be done.

The purpose of Decision Analysis is to identify what needs to be done, develop the specific criteria for its accomplishment, evaluate the available alternatives relative to those criteria, and identify the risks involved.

For the remainder of this chapter, we will explain the major elements in the process of Decision Analysis and show how the process is used. Our example involves a relatively simple, straightforward choice among four possible courses of action.

The Major Elements of Decision Analysis

The Decision Statement

In Problem Analysis we begin with a *deviation statement,* which names the situation to be resolved. In Decision Analysis we will begin with the *decision statement,* or name of the decision.

In Problem Analysis, resolution consisted of a verifiable answer to the question "Why?" In Decision Analysis, resolution will consist of an answer to the questions "To what purpose?" "Which?" and "How?"

A decision statement provides the focus for everything that follows and sets the limits of the choice. The criteria to be developed will follow from it, describing in detail the requirements of the decision. The alternatives will be judged on their ability to meet these requirements. Because the decision statement sets all these activities in motion, it has another quality in common with the deviation statement: *the way it is worded deserves careful attention.*

A decision statement always indicates some kind of action and its intended result: "Select a New Director of Quality Control" or "Devise a New Personnel Evaluation System." It also indicates the *level* at which the decision is to be made. In the case we presented earlier—the "need to increase the research and development capabilities of this organization"—the decision failed chiefly because no thought was given to the *level* of the decision. The statement of purpose gave the decision-making team no guidance and set no limits, up or down, on the range of alternatives that would be considered. The only stage it set was one on which an alternative-driven solution could assume the starring role.

The Objectives for the Decision

Objectives, in our terminology, are the criteria for the decision—the specific details of what the decision is to accomplish. We establish these objectives once we state the purpose of the decision and agree upon the level at which it is to be made. We do this before discussing alternatives, sometimes even before identifying alternatives. Decision Analysis is the antithesis of identifying a course of action and then building a case to support it. Instead we are moving from what needs to be accomplished toward the alternative that can best accomplish it. For example, if we want to hire a new executive, we are more likely to make a good choice if we *first* identify the qualities of an ideal candidate and *then* begin the interviewing process. No experienced manager needs to have this reasoning spelled out. Objectives are clear measures of the ends we want to achieve, for only with clear measures can we make reasoned choices.

Musts and Wants

We divide the objectives into two categories: MUSTS and WANTS. The MUST objectives are mandatory: they *must* be achieved to guarantee a successful decision. When the time comes to assess alternatives against our objectives, any alternative that cannot fulfill a MUST objective will immediately drop out of the analysis. These objectives must be measurable because they function as a screen to eliminate failure-prone alternatives. We must be able to say, "This alternative *absolutely* cannot fulfill this objective; it cannot meet a requirement that is mandatory for success." For example, a typical MUST objective in a hiring decision is "Two years' experience as supervisor in this industry." If that length of experience is mandatory, then there is no point in considering any candidate who hasn't put in the two years. It is a measurable objective: A candidate either has it or doesn't have it. His or her *other* good qualities are irrelevant.

All other objectives are categorized as WANTS. The alternatives we generate will be judged on their *relative* performance against WANT objectives, not on whether or not they fulfill them. The function of these objectives is to give us a comparative picture of alternatives—*a sense of how the alternatives perform relative to each other*.

A WANT objective may be mandatory but cannot be classified as a MUST for one or two reasons: First, it may not be measurable. It cannot, therefore, give us an absolute Yes-or-No judgment about the performance of an alternative. Secondly, we may not want a Yes-or-No judgment. We may prefer to use that objective as a *relative* measure of performance.

An objective will be stated frequently as a MUST and then be rephrased as a WANT so that it can perform both functions. For example, "Two years' experience in this industry" (MUST) may be rephrased as "Maximum experience in this industry" (WANT). Now, when we come to evaluate the alternatives, we can make two kinds of judgments: Candidates with less than two years' experience will be eliminated. The remaining candidates will be judged relative to each other on the basis of their experience.

Here is an example of a high-priority objective that could *not* be used as a MUST: "Interacts well with managers at all levels." No matter how important this objective may be, it concerns an ability that can be measured only in a relative way. All four job candidates may meet this objective *but only one will meet it best*. This is exactly what we want to know: who meets it *best*? We do not want to know who meets it *at all*—a judgment reserved for a MUST objective. A WANT objective is not necessarily less important than a MUST; it simply serves a different purpose.

Someone once succinctly described the functions of these two kinds of objectives by saying, "The MUSTS decide who gets to play, but the WANTS decide who wins."

Alternatives

An ideal alternative perfectly fulfills every condition set for it without adding new difficulties. Unfortunately, ideal alternatives are rare. We must, therefore, evaluate each available alternative by measuring it against all of our objectives. It is the relative quality of that fit that concerns us.

If we must choose among several alternatives, we will have to decide which one will best fulfill our objectives with the smallest acceptable risk. In other words, we try to make a *balanced choice*. An alternative that best accomplishes the objectives but carries severe risks is not, after all, the best choice. Another alternative, perhaps less exciting but safer, may be the best balanced choice.

If there is only one alternative, we must decide whether it is good enough to accept. In this case our evaluation will focus on its relative worth compared with a perfect but unobtainable alternative.

If we must choose between a current and a proposed course of action, then we consider both to be alternatives. We evaluate their performance against our objectives just as we would if both had been proposed. Whatever is currently being done is, after all, an alternative; the choice is whether to continue that way or find another, better way.

If, in the absence of *any* alternative, we must create something new, we can usually build an alternative from available components. We then choose the best and most feasible combinations, treat each as a separate alternative, and evaluate all of them against an ideal model of an alternative.

In the next chapter we will examine true examples of these situations and explore the sources of alternatives.

The Consequences of the Choice

The final step in Decision Analysis is the search for possible adverse consequences of all feasible alternatives.

The negative consequences of any action are as tangible as its benefits, sometimes more so. Once a decision has been made and implemented, any of its negative effects will eventually become real problems. The effects of decisions, good or bad, always outlive the decision-making process that produced them. And which effects, good or bad, are longest remembered? "The evil that men do," wrote Shakespeare, "lives after them, the good is oft interred with their bones. . . ." Some things don't change at all in almost four hundred years.

We must thoroughly explore and evaluate the possible adverse consequences of any alternative *before* we make a final decision. This is the only opportunity we will ever have to deal with such effects at no cost beyond a little intellectual effort. We must recognize possible adverse consequences before they occur, and take them into consideration as part of our decision. Having recognized and assessed them, we may be able to avoid them altogether or take steps in the present that will reduce their effect in the future. A risk attached to an alternative is not necessarily a totally damning factor—*provided that someone sees it while there is time to do something about it.* Any evaluation and choice that omits a disciplined, systematic search for potential negative consequences is an invitation to disaster.

Decision Analysis seldom deals with certainties. The further into the future a proposed action extends, the less certain it can be. It is because of these uncertainties that the process of Decision Analysis depends on our judgments, evaluations, experience, and intuitive feelings. All of these supply the valid data we need to support the correct decision we must make.

To set aside feelings, instincts, and the inner voice that says, "I don't feel right about this . . ." is to throw away a valuable resource. It leads to such errors as hiring a person you don't like and can't work with just because "the resume looked so good, and I was trying to be objective." That is not good decision making. A good decision is one that will work. Overlooking factors that make a choice unworkable is a fundamental mistake. A reasonable selection and a good decision always depend on thorough study and careful evaluation of *all* relevant information.

Decision Analysis is a methodical, systematic process. But it is also as creative and innovative a process as its users choose to make it.

The Techniques of Decision Analysis

The following situation illustrates the use of Decision Analysis techniques. It concerns selection of one source of a needed service from among several potential suppliers.

The Decision Statement

Our client's decision statement was: "Select the Best Personnel Information System for [Our] Corporation." The people involved in making this decision were the Vice President for Operations, the Vice President for Personnel, the Director of Information Systems, and one of the firm's attorneys. They worked as a team to decide three things: the level of the decision, who was to delegate necessary research tasks to subordinates, and who was to use the resulting information to reach the final conclusion. The team was not involved in the research required to make the evaluation.

Operating this way, the team arrived at its conclusion after three one-hour sessions held over a period of two weeks.

Compared with previous, similar decision situations, this was considered a tremendous saving of time and effort.

The decision statement indicated not only the purpose of the decision but the level at which it would be made. It set the stage for the *kinds* of alternatives that would be considered. Had the statement been worded: "Improve Our Method of Personnel Information Recording and Reporting," the character of the decision would have been different: the selection of a new system would have appeared as one of several alternatives—not at all what the team wanted.

A decision statement is, in a way, the product of previous decisions. The team had already decided that it wanted a new system to replace all the present methods and procedures. Thus, the wording of the decision statement immediately vetoed a dozen other possible decisions that might have been made.

The Objectives for the Decision

What *must* the new system do? What would the team *like* it to do in addition? What constraints affect the choice of a new system? Such are the questions that every team of decision makers has to ask in order to begin setting objectives. The answers to these questions will result in a list of objectives. The objectives will then be classified as MUSTS or WANTS.

Among our client's MUST objectives for the new personnel information reporting system were these:

MUST be capable of . . .

● Regional Equal Employment Opportunity (EEO) reporting

● Reporting to management, using Report Writer

● Capturing and reporting salary and job history

Each of these was considered mandatory, and each was measurable: either a system could offer these features or it could not.

The list of WANT objectives represented additional desirable but not mandatory criteria. Following are five of the seventeen WANT objectives that appeared in the analysis:

● Implementation six months after start

● Written in COBOL

- Occupational Safety and Health Administration (OSHA) reporting capability

- Elimination of multiple forms by using turn-around document

- Security

Weighting the Objectives

Once the WANT objectives had been identified, each one was weighted according to its relative importance. The *most* important objective was identified and given a weight of 10. All other objectives were then weighted in comparison with the first, from 10 (equally important) down to a possible 1 (not very important).

No attempt was made to rank the objectives. The purpose of the 10–1 weighting scale was simply to make visible the relationships among these objectives: What mattered most? What could be done without, if necessary?

When the time comes to evaluate the alternatives, we do so by assessing them *relative to each other* against all WANT objectives—one at a time. This is why it is critical at the outset to identify the most important objectives. It is pointless to know that a particular alternative satisfies nine out of ten WANT objectives if, in fact, it is the tenth that is most crucial to success of the decision. We must also examine the *balance* of WANT objectives and look for certain danger signals:

- Too many high numbers may indicate either unrealistic expectations or a faulty perception of which objectives can guarantee success.

- Too many low numbers suggest that unimportant details may be smothering the analysis.

- Too many objectives reflecting the vested interest of a single department may lead to an unworkable decision. This is especially true if other departments are equally affected by the final decision.

- Loaded objectives—those that guarantee a smooth passage for a certain alternative and blackball all others—can make a mockery of an analysis.

These are the weights our client team assigned to the five WANT objectives:

- Implementation six months after start 10
- Written in COBOL 9
- OSHA reporting capability 8
- Elimination of multiple forms by using turnaround document 5
- Security 3

Generating and Evaluating Alternatives

In this case, alternatives were fairly clear-cut: The team identified four leading suppliers of the system they wanted and then launched the evaluation.

Evaluation of Alternatives Against MUST Objectives

In this evaluation an alternative either meets all the MUST objectives (GO) or does not (NO GO). A NO GO is immediately dropped from further consideration.

The MUSTS, you may remember, were:

- Regional Equal Employment Opportunity (EEO) reporting
- Reporting to management, using Report Writer
- Capturing and reporting salary and job history

To the surprise of most people on the team, one highly regarded system failed at this point. It could not provide the Report Writer feature. The alternatives are shown in Figure 6, which appears on pages 94–95.

Note that the information columns in Figure 6 tell us *why* an alternative has passed or failed. By listing this information, the process has become visible. Facts, opinions, and judgments are on record. A written summary exists for future reference, leaving nothing to be memorized or forgotten. And necessary information is available for anyone who must approve the final decision.

Having eliminated Company D, the team now carried the three remaining alternatives into the next phase: comparative evaluation on the basis of the WANT objectives.

Beginning with the first WANT objective—"Implementation six months after start" (weight of 10)—the team evaluated the information it had gathered about Companies A, B, and C.

Company A had given an estimate of six months; Company B, six months; Company C, four months. The estimates from Companies A and C seemed reliable. The Vice President of Operations was less certain about Company B. He had heard that two of B's customers had reported slightly delayed implementation; otherwise, they were satisfied with the service they had received.

Based on this information, the team decided that Company C, with a reliable estimate of four months, *best* met the implementation objective. They gave Company C a score of 10 on that objective, and gave relatives scores of 9 to Company A and 8 to Company B. What purpose do these numbers serve? *They help to reflect our judgments.*

At this point in the analysis, all objectives have been sorted out and made visible, and the WANTS have been weighted. Now the alternatives will be sorted out, permitting us to judge the relative advantages of each alternative. For example, how good an implementation job can Company C do *compared with Companies A and B?* As each company is evaluated on the basis of all the WANT objectives, its relative overall performance and ability to produce desirable results will gradually become clear.

Figure 6.

Alternatives Evaluated

MUST OBJECTIVES	COMPANY A INFO	GO/NO GO	COMPANY B INFO	GO/NO GO
EEO reporting	Yes—meets Gov't requirement; more detail using GRS.	GO	Yes—meets Gov't requirement; more detail using Report Writer.	GO
Report Writer	Yes—all reports are printed using Report Writer.	GO	Standard reports use Report Writer on call.	GO
Capture/report salary and job history	Yes—as many as we want using CEH	GO	Yes—can generate as many as we want into system.	GO

Figure 7, on pages 96–97, shows the judgments the team made of the relative performances of the three alternatives, scored against all of the WANT objectives.

People sometimes are bothered when none of the alternatives seems to deserve a 10. They are even more disturbed when none of the alternatives performs well on a particular objective. We give a 10 to the alternative that comes *closest* to meeting the objective, and score the other alternatives *relative to it*. It is not an ideal that we seek through this comparative evaluation. What we seek is an answer to the question: "Of these (real and attainable) alternatives, which best fulfills the objective?"

There is one caution: If, during the scoring step, a statement such as "none of the alternatives is much good" comes up repeatedly from one objective to the next, then something is obviously wrong. The objectives are unrealistic, and no *real and attainable* alternative can fulfill them. But this is a rare circumstance. People in a decision-making position are usually there because they have a good grasp of what is feasible; they do not devise unattainable objectives.

At the other extreme, all alternatives may perform well on nearly all objectives. This is caused by a set of objectives so loose that any of a number of similar alternatives will be equally good at satisfying the requirements of the decision. The simple remedy is to go back to the list of WANT objectives and make them tighter, more demanding, and more numerous. The alternative that really does offer more can then stand out.

Against Must Objectives

COMPANY C INFO	GO/NO GO	COMPANY D INFO	GO/NO GO
Yes—meets Gov't requirement; more detail using Report Writer.	GO	Yes—meets Gov't requirement; standard report.	GO
Standard reports use Report Writer for on-call report per pass.	GO	No Report Writer.	NO GO
Yes—unlimited.	GO	—	

Now we need answers to two questions: How does each alternative perform across the board? How does it stack up against each of the other alternatives on total performance against WANT objectives? We can answer by computing the weighted scores of each alternative.

A *weighted score* is the score of an alternative multiplied by the weight of the objective to which the score refers. For example:

> Company A scored 9 on the WANT objective "Implementation six months after start." That objective has a weight of 10. Therefore the *weighted score* of Company A on that objective is 90 (9 x 10).

We continue by computing Company A's weighted scores for *all* the WANT objectives. Then we add up all of the weighted scores to produce the *total weighted score* for the Company A alternative. We complete this step by repeating the procedure for the other alternatives, producing the results that appear in Figure 8, pages 98–99.

The total weighted scores function as *visible comparative measurements* of the alternatives. Their numbers indicate that one alternative is more viable than the others, that one course of action is apparently more workable than the others. There is nothing magical about the numbers. A base of 10-to-1, for both

---

Figure 7.

Alternatives Evaluated

WANT OBJECTIVES	WEIGHT	COMPANY A INFO	SCORE
Implementation 6 months after start	10	Yes—6 months.	9
Written in COBOL	9	Yes—with called sub-routines required.	9
OSHA Reporting	8	Required Gov't Reporting; most flexible.	10
Elimination of multiple forms by using turnaround document	5	Yes—minimum number forms & Cust. Des. Document.	10
Security	3	Will do what is necessary to solve problem. Also password security in Report Writer.	10

the weighting of WANT objectives and the scoring of alternatives, is a simple, logical, and productive means for producing good results.

As Figure 8 indicates, the total weighted scores were 331 for Company A, 271 for Company B, and 328 for Company C. As we have said, this is a sampling of the full-blown analysis that included seventeen WANT objectives. For the record, the complete scores were: 1009 for Company A, 752 for Company B, and 878 for Company C. Company A, then, satisfied the objectives of the decision to a greater degree than either of its competitors.

Under certain conditions we can vary the way we assign numerical weights. If a manager must work with fifty or a hundred objectives, for example, he or she may break these down into categories, with a weight (or percentage of influence) given to each category. In this instance, a single WANT objective may bear a weight of 10, but belong to a category with a comparatively low weight. While the logic of the Decision Analysis process remains unchanged, this modification of technique reflects the particular requirements of the decision.

The Tentative Choice

The total weighted score gives us a tool for selecting a *tentative choice*. Although the tentative choice often graduates to

Against Want Objectives

COMPANY B INFO	SCORE	COMPANY C INFO	SCORE
Yes—6 months. (They say?)	8	Yes—4 months	10
Yes—called sub-routines & conversion to B6700.	8	Yes—no called sub-routines required.	10
Required Gov't Reporting.	8	Required Gov't Reporting.	9
Yes—minimum number of forms & standard document.	8	Yes—minimum number of forms.	9
No security on Data File. Must do ourselves.	5	Password security in Report Writer.	7

the status of *final* choice, it should never do so before we explore the potential risks involved. Two decades of experience have shown us clearly that elimination of this final step of Decision Analysis—because "one alternative is so obviously the leader"—can negate the value of all work done up to that point.

The Consequences of Alternatives

If it is so important to explore potential risks, why do people often fail to do it? There are several understandable reasons. If an analysis of three alternatives produces total weighted scores of 700, 350, and 210, it may seem a waste of time to brainstorm for potential risks. In another case someone may be reluctant to inject pessimism into the enthusiasm of "We've done all this work! And we've produced this great alternative!" That one doubtful member of an optimistic decision-making team may very well hide those negative opinions. One last and very common reason for dropping the step of risk exploration is this: We are often unable or unwilling to apply the lessons of the

Figure 8.

Alternatives and Their

WANT OBJECTIVES	WEIGHT	COMPANY A INFO	SCORE	WEIGHTED SCORE
Implementation 6 months after start	10	Yes—6 months	9	90
Written in COBOL	9	Yes—with called sub-routines required.	9	81
OSHA Reporting	8	Required Gov't Reporting; most flexible.	10	80
Elimination of multiple forms by using turnaround document	5	Yes—minimum number Forms & Cust. Des. Document	10	50
Security	3	Will do what is necessary to solve problem. Also password security in Report Writer.	10	30
Total Weighted Scores:				331

past to the decisions of today. One manager told us that, early in his career, he had meekly suggested to his boss that the potential problems of an alternative under consideration had not been adequately considered. Even more meekly he reminded his boss that a decision made in another department had seriously backfired several months before. "That," his boss replied scornfully, "was *them* and *then* And this is *us* and *now*." The subject was dropped. The decision proved to be a good one, but that did not prove the young manager wrong. A year or two after a decision is implemented, nobody regrets the time spent probing for its risks. It is a mere fraction of the time spent in regret over a risk that should have been explored but was not.

In the earlier steps of Decision Analysis we try to make our objectives as comprehensive as possible, and our evaluation of alternatives as rigorous as possible. But these activities go just so far. They must be followed by the most creative and difficult step in the process: *considering the consequences of alternatives*. This entails answering at least these five questions:

Total Weighted Scores

COMPANY B INFO	SCORE	WEIGHTED SCORE	COMPANY C INFO	SCORE	WEIGHTED SCORE
Yes—6 months (They say?)	8	80	Yes—4 months	10	100
Yes—called sub-routines & conversion to B6700 required.	8	72	Yes—no called sub-routines required.	10	90
Required Gov't Reporting	8	64	Required Gov't Reporting	9	72
Yes—minimum number of forms & standard document	8	40	Yes—minimum number of forms.	9	45
No security on Data Files. Must do ourselves.	5	15	Password security in Report Writer.	7	21
		271			328

If we choose *this* alternative:

- What requirements for success have we missed in the previous stages of this analysis?

- What factors within the organization, based on our experience, could harm its acceptance or its implementation?

- What kinds of changes within the organization could harm its long-range success?

- What kinds of external changes (such as competitor activity and government regulations) could harm its long-range success?

- What kinds of things tend to cause problems in implementing this type of decision?

In this step of the process, we try to destroy our best alternatives one at a time. We become destructive, negative, and pessimistic. The degree to which managers accept this process is largely determined by the amount of their experience. Experience teaches us that there are no awards for past optimism over current failures. This fact is borne out by the impossibility of finding out who, in any organization, was really responsible for the very worst decisions that were ever made.

We begin this step with the *tentative* choice—the alternative with the highest total weighted score. We examine it by itself. We examine its probabilities of failure or potential trouble. Remember that this is *never* an exercise in comparisons. We do *not* say, "Alternative A is more likely to produce this problem than Alternative B." Comparison is not a useful approach. Each alternative must be examined separately.

We then rate the adverse consequences of an alternative on the basis of *probability and seriousness:* What is the probability that this (adverse consequence) will occur? If it (the adverse consequence) does occur, how serious will it be? We can use ratings of High, Medium, and Low (H,M,L) or a scale of 10 (highly probable/very serious) to 1 (unlikely/not at all serious). The 10-to-1 system is fine—provided that we avoid the temptation to start multiplying: "Probability of 9 x Seriousness of 3 = 27." (We did this in our first book, *The Rational Manager,* and went on to add these numbers for each alternative. This produced "adverse consequence totals" for all the alternatives. We have found over the years that this is not useful information.) If we permit the numbers to obscure the information that produced them, we can lose sight of the serious adverse consequences.

We will not lose any sleep over an adverse consequence of low probability and minimal significance. But we will be *very* attentive if an adverse consequence is considered both highly probable and very serious.

Following are some adverse consequences that were identified during the final step of the Personnel Information System decision.

COMPANY A: Rumor: Company may sell out within three years, causing severe disruption of service.
Probability?   Medium
Seriousness   High
if it occurs?

COMPANY B: High turnover. Key people with greatest knowledge of our account leave vendor's employ.
Probability?   Medium
Seriousness   Medium
if it occurs?

COMPANY C: If they have few experienced employees, C may not be able to meet our future needs.
Probability?   Low
Seriousness   Medium
if it occurs?

Three factors determine the number and importance of potential adverse consequences that are identified for the alternatives: the extent of their existence, our ability to find them, and our willingness to address those we find.

How useful is the Decision Analysis process if potential adverse consequences can knock out the very alternative that scored highest on objectives we worked so hard to develop? It is *because* of the previous steps in the process, the visibility of information, and the tracking of our thinking from the decision statement to this point that we can best assess the potential adverse consequences. It is only now, with all the data before us, that we can stretch our imaginations beyond the body of facts we have amassed, survey it all, and ask: "What did we miss?"

The outcome of this particular case was that our client chose to go with Company C, the runner-up in the numerical scoring. Someone had picked up a rumor that Company A might sell out within the next three years. The rumor was never substantiated but was there just the same. Moreover,

Company C's youth and relatively small size seemed to offer at least as many potential advantages as disadvantages. Its management team was aggressive, ambitious, and preoccupied with service as a means of getting and retaining new business. Our client's service needs were unlikely to outstrip Company C's ability to meet them. The team made the best decision possible based on the experience and judgment of the team members and all available information.

So how did it all turn out?

Company A did not sell out within three years. But by that time its reputation for service had been eclipsed—by Company C, the team's choice. Company C did an excellent job. It had the system in full operation within four months as promised, and continued to treat our client as a key customer. The decision-making team remained satisfied that it had made the right choice, and never regretted having taken the rumor about Company A into its deliberations.

In three one-hour sessions, conducted over a period of two weeks, the team had reached a prudent decision that produced exactly the results they had hoped for: a balanced, reasoned choice of action that all could subscribe to and support—a *choice that worked* for the organization.

Chapter Summary

Through the process of Decision Analysis, we expand from a concise statement of purpose to a number of criteria for completely defining the achievement of that purpose. These criteria permit us to judge available alternatives on specific issues. Then, by narrowing those judgments through summarization and a systematic method of evaluation and notation, we reach a final conclusion.

The power of the process lies in the ability it gives managers to make *productive* use of all available information and judgments. The process does not guarantee that perfect decisions will be made every time. Given human fallibility and the usual inadequacy of available information, there will always be errors. At the very least, however, the process of Decision Analysis enables the manager to reduce the incidence of errors by providing a systematic framework for evaluating alternatives. Going beyond this simplest level of efficiency, the examples in the next chapter illustrate how much more effective Decision Analysis can be when creative and innovative managers apply the basic logic of the process to their most important choices.

CHAPTER 5

The Uses of Decision Analysis

Introduction: Types of Decisions

Every decision we make requires us to think in terms of *objectives, alternatives,* and *potential risks.* That choice may involve a thousand criteria plus the inputs and deliberations of a hundred or more people. Or it may involve only five criteria and ten minutes of deliberation by one person. The dimensions are immaterial because the basic process is always the same. And the final judgment is always: "This is what ought to be done."

In this chapter we will describe how managers have applied the systematic process of Decision Analysis. The true cases we cite illustrate individual approaches to the development and evaluation of objectives, alternatives, and potential risks in a number of common decision-making situations. In each case a manager or management team has scaled and modified the procedure to match specific requirements.

These decision situations fall into five categories:

- The complex decision that requires examination of a large amount of information, and involves the judgments of many people.

- The "Yes/No" decision that involves only two alternatives: to take or reject a course of action; to do something in a different way or continue as before.

- The decision as to whether a single proposed course of action is sound enough to be implemented.

- The decision in which an original alternative must be developed by the decision-maker or team.

- The routine decision: hiring, purchase of equipment or services, development of personnel policies, and other everyday decisions.

A final section is devoted to *adverse consequence thinking*—the protection of decisions.

The Complex Decision

This example, illustrating full and detailed use of Decision Analysis, clearly demonstrates each step in the thinking process.

Our client operates one of the world's largest underground mines. In the company's primary mining (its first cut-through), it takes out about 40% of the ore. The remainder is left behind as pillars to prevent collapse of the tunnels. In the secondary stage, the tunnels are filled in to support the ceilings and the pillars are mined out. This is critical, dangerous work: A mistake can result in trapped miners as well as loss of a great deal of ore. The best way of backfilling and mining out the pillars depends on the specific characteristics of the mine, the ore, and the surrounding strata. How this is done never is treated as a cut-and-dried decision; it always entails close evaluation of many possibilities.

The company had to make a decision concerning removal of pillars on the 2500- and 2800-foot levels. About $200 million in ore remained underground. Two methods had been suggested: "sub-level cave" and "high rise with sub-level cave." Both were sound, accepted practices; neither method had an apparent advantage over the other. Since opinions of the top technical people were about evenly divided between the two alternatives, the organization named a task force of thirteen to study the situation and arrive at a decision. Among them were senior production people, geologists, safety engineers, ventilation and scheduling personnel, and cost control personnel. Each group of experts on the team had a somewhat different point of view and knowledge of the business.

They first discussed the conditions required for successful pillar removal. They recognized that there were four groups of considerations. These were listed as: "Metal Recovery," "Mining Conditions," "Cost," and "Operation." From these four groupings, they developed twenty specific objectives for the decision. These included: "maximum metal recovery," "minimum siltstone in ore," "safety," "least cost per metal unit," and "minimum cement in ore stream." With these as an ideal model of a perfect removal procedure, they began to evaluate the two available methods. Each method was evaluated against each criterion to determine which came closer to the ideal. They considered all aspects of the two methods point by point, using a numerical system to record and keep track of the judgments they made as they went along.

When they had finished evaluating the relative advantages of the two methods, they found that the "sub-level cave" procedure appeared to be 25% better than the "high rise" method. Even the proponents of "sub-level cave" were surprised at the degree to which it outperformed "high rise."

The team then looked at the adverse consequences of adopting each method. They found that the "high rise" alternative carried somewhat more penalty and risk than the other. The choice was clear: The "sub-level cave" method more nearly approximated the ideal and carried fewer potential penalties. That method was put into operation, and the $200 million in ore was recovered without incident. Their analysis, excluding information on adverse consequences, is outlined in Figure 9, pages 106–109.

Summary

This is an interesting example because, at the outset, even the experts could not see any marked advantage of one method over the other. They had preferences, but no one ever suggested that either method was dangerous, unsound, or even inadequate. After the experts had considered and clarified the exact conditions for successful pillar removal, however, they were able to evaluate the two methods *in detail, relative to each other, against an ideal.* As a result they found a decided difference between the two.

This is nearly always the outcome in such a situation. When there is too much detail to juggle mentally, some systematic way must be found to evaluate the many judgments

Figure 9.

Select a Mining Method for

OBJECTIVES

MUST
Meet schedule
Retain stability 18c Sub
Be profitable

WANT	WEIGHT
Maximum metal recovery	10
Minimum cost/metal per ton	10
Provide safe mining conditions with regard to ringfirers, brow firers	10
Confidence in success taking into account fill and stability of structures	10
Good ventilation conditions	8
Maximum flexibility of production	8
Maximum recovery of metal in rib pillars	8
Defer advance south of primary stopes	7

(*continued on pages 108–109*)

the 2500–2800 Orebody Pillars

ALTERNATIVES

SUB-LEVEL CAVE		HIGH RISE WITH SUB-LEVEL CAVE	
INFORMATION	**GO/NO GO**	**INFORMATION**	**GO/NO GO**
On present schedule	GO	Alternative schedule but would need some tons from 2G/2B block	GO
Ref. JPD/OPS MIN 4.2	GO	Ref. SBL/RCM MIN 4.2	GO
Memo reference JL/2.1/MIN 8.10.2 November 1	GO	Memo reference FoS/2.1/MIN 8.10.3 dated October 29	GO

INFORMATION	SCORE	WEIGHTED SCORE	INFORMATION	SCORE	WEIGHTED SCORE
186,000 tons	10	100	177,000 tons	9	90
$288/ton	7	70	$190/ton	10	100
Least exposure for men	10	100	Moderate exposure	7	70
Least reliance on fill and stability of structures	10	100	Some reliance on fill and stability	5	50
No problems	10	80	Need to get fresh air to the hanging wall through pillars and cement drives	7	56
Multiple draw points required	10	80	Few draw points available	7	56
More problems due to ribs being surrounded by cement fill on two sides and unconsolidated fill on two sides	7	56	Less unconsolidated fill surrounding rib pillars	10	80
No problems	10	70	Would require primary stopes earlier than using sub-level cave	2	14

Figure 9 concluded

OBJECTIVES

WANT	WEIGHT	
Ensure simplicity of operation	5	
Minimum development in fill	5	
Minimum siltstone in ore stream	5	
Minimum manpower requirement	4	
Minimum development footage	4	
Minimum equipment requirements	4	
Maximum use of available equipment	3	
With least casual water	2	
With best roadways	2	
Minimum cement in ore stream	1	
TOTAL		

SUB-LEVEL CAVE			HIGH RISE WITH SUB-LEVEL CAVE		
INFORMATION	SCORE	WEIGHTED SCORE	INFORMATION	SCORE	WEIGHTED SCORE
Repeated straight-forward operation	10	50	Some complications	7	35
No development needed	10	50	4000 feet of development in fill	1	5
Would tend to get more through dilution in the cave	8	40	Minimum	10	50
Some extra requirements	8	32	Would expect more tons/manshift	10	40
Refer memo JL/2.1/MIN 8.10.2	8	32	Refer memo FoS/2.1/MIN 8.10.3	10	40
More drilling equipment required	9	36	Minimum	10	40
Minimum special demands	10	30	Will need small load haul dump units for development through fill and also may need special support equipment	8	24
Water will drain and not necessarily be on production subs	10	20	More washing out water as in open stopes	7	14
Good roadways	10	20	Fill provides poor roadways when affected by water	8	16
Minimum cement	10	10	More mining through cement	8	8
		976			788

that have to be made. We have to remember that the human computer in all of us, no matter how overloaded, will stagger along, doing the best it can. But "doing the best it can" may not be good enough. In our example, the managers helped their own cranial computers by breaking down their task into steps and taking each step in turn.

The mining decision involved hundreds of separate technical considerations, and thousands of independent judgments were made in the course of the deliberations. Yet none of this information was lost. It was gathered into categories and groups of judgments and made visible. These summary evaluations then were pulled together into an overall evaluation of the two methods. Next, the adverse consequences were studied. Finally, all judgments were integrated into a single judgment to answer the question: "*On balance,* comparing the two alternatives, how well does each perform against the defined set of necessary conditions?"

A decision arrived at through Decision Analysis may sound no different from one produced through reflection based on experience and without a systematic process. But the validity of the former is a thousand times greater, for all elements that go into the decision remain accessible and visible. The decision can be reconstructed logically in all its detail. Every step in thinking and in dealing with information can be shown and duplicated. This allows for error-checking and for augmentation as new information becomes available. And it simplifies communication and explanation of the decision. As has been shown, anyone outside the decision team, asking why the "sub-level cave" method was judged 25% better than the other, can be shown point by point exactly why this is so. If objectives are correct and facts accurate, then the conclusion is unarguable—particularly in the eyes of an expert.

Yes or No?
Should We Take or Reject a Course of Action?

When managers first are introduced to Decision Analysis, they learn to use its techniques through the kinds of examples we have presented. Objectives are set, alternatives are identified and evaluated, risks are examined. After managers become familiar with the basic procedure, one of the first concerns they raise goes something like this: "That's all well and good if you have three or four alternatives to choose from. But most of the time my real-life judgments are going to consist of Yes or No. What good is Decision Analysis when the choice is that limited?"

Nowhere is the Yes/No decision more prevalent than in government bureaucracies. And nowhere is the necessity of communicating the background of a decision so important.

The following letter was written by an executive of the Department of Natural Resources for a state in the southern United States. It was addressed to the Director of the Bureau of Pollution Control in a city located in that state. The city had proposed a plan for managing the water quality of the river on which it is located. It is the responsibility of the Department of Natural Resources to accept or reject such proposals. Yes/No decisions are indeed the reality of the job for the Department in all these cases, and the Department uses Decision Analysis to approach all such decisions as well as to reach and communicate its conclusions.

Dear Mr. _____:

This letter is written in response to the request in your [date] letter for a detailed written explanation of [our] rejection of the proposal for storage of effluence as a part of the overall plan to meet X River standards.

Since this is a very complex issue, we attempted to be as systematic and comprehensive as possible in considering positive and negative aspects of the concept and in anticipating its impacts. We started with the following decision statement: To decide whether the concept of flow variable wastewater discharges to the X River from City of Y facilities is acceptable.

We then identified objectives that should apply for any water quality control strategy for the X River. These objectives were separated into MUST objectives and WANT objectives. To be a MUST, the objective has to be both measurable and mandatory. If an objective is not both measurable and mandatory, it is a WANT. To each WANT objective, we assigned a weight signifying its importance or desirability, on a scale of 1 to 10, with 10 being the maximum importance of desirability. The objectives we identified are listed below.

MUST Objectives

1. Meet existing water quality standards in the X River.

2. Is equitable for all types of discharges to the X River.

3. Maintain a minimum reserve capacity of 15% for ultimate oxygen demand at all flows in the X River.

WANT Objectives	Weight
1. Provide protection for potential water supplies downstream.	10
2. Maximize water quality in the X River.	8
3. Maximize reliability of wastewater treatment control systems.	8
4. Minimize present worth of treatment/control systems.	8
5. Minimize organic loading to River and Reservoir.	7
6. Minimize nutrient (nitrogen and phosphorus) loading to Reservoir.	7
7. Maximize enforceability of effluent standards for treatment/control systems.	4
8. Increase reserve capacity for ultimate oxygen demand.	4
9. Do not delay the construction grants process.	4
10. Make optimal use of X River waste assimilative capacity.	3

All these objectives are not necessarily compatible with each other, but they are rational objectives that should be considered. The weights for each objective were the consensus of our highest levels of management and most experienced staff members.

The next step in our decision process was to identify alternatives and to determine how well each alternative would satisfy the objectives. (Note: The MUSTS are not weighted because any alternative not satisfying every MUST is unacceptable; we seek an alternative that will satisfy all MUSTS and that will satisfy WANTS better than the other alternatives.) In this case, we have only two alternatives to consider: Yes, the concept of flow variable discharge is acceptable; and No, the concept is unacceptable.

The No alternative satisfies all MUSTS; it is equivalent to saying that the waste load allocations determined for all X River discharges and transmitted to the City in our letter of [date] will be followed. These allocations will allow water quality standards to be met, they are equitable for all discharges, and they provide a 15% reserve assimilative capacity.

The Yes alternative would have a number of technical questions to be resolved (such as the specifics of an equitable policy, since other governments would have to be allowed the option of flow variable discharge; and the specific allowable discharges from all point waste sources of the range of X River flows). We assumed that the technical questions could be resolved; thus, it was considered that the Yes alternative could be made to satisfy the MUST objectives.

In comparing how well the alternatives would satisfy the WANTS, one could assign a score, say, on a scale of 1 to 10, for each alternative at each WANT, then multiply by the weight of each WANT and get a total weighted score for each alternative. Or, one could simply signify the relative merits of an alternative by positive and negative signs. (This was done, for example by [Company] in its ABC Water Quality Management Plan.)

By either method, the end product in this case is the same. The No alternative satisfies all WANTS better than the Yes alternative, except for WANTS 4, 5 and 10. The No alternative is superior to the Yes alternative on WANTS 1, 2, 6, and 8 basically because there will be lesser loadings of most pollutants discharged. The No alternative is superior on WANTS 3, 7, and 9 because it will result in a system that is less complex to design, operate, monitor, and control. The extensive technical work that would be needed before engineering could commence for the Yes alternative would mean significant delays in the completion of the Y City Facilities Plans. The Yes and No alternatives rank about equally for WANT 5: the amounts of phosphorus discharged would be the same. However, the No alternative might be somewhat more favorable since a lesser loading of total nitrogen might be possible, and since upgrading existing systems now might make

it easier to effect phosphorus removal if found
necessary in the future. The Yes alternative is
superior on WANTS 4 and 10, since it would almost surely have a lower present worth and since
it would obviously make more use of natural
assimilative capacity of the River.

The final step in our decision process was to
identify and compare the adverse consequences of
implementing either alternative. We identified
eight such consequences and tried to quantify
the probability [P] and seriousness [S] of each.
This again was done on a scale of 1 to 10, with
1 representing very low probability and
seriousness and 10 representing very high probability and seriousness. The results follow.

	Adverse Consequences	Yes		No	
		P	S	P	S
1.	Delays in the grants process for all [State] facilities	10	9	8	3
2.	Loss of momentum	7	8	3	8
3.	Difficulty in enforcing effluent standards	9	3	4	3
4.	Adverse effects on Z Reservoir	5	7	3	3
5.	Non-acceptance by City of G	1	7	6	7
6.	Non-acceptance by other local governments	8	8	1	8
7.	Non-acceptance by [United States Environmental Protection Agency]	9	10	1	10
8.	Non-acceptance by environmentalist groups	9	9	1	9

The values assigned for probability and seriousness, like the weights for WANT objectives or
the scores for alternatives satisfying each
WANT, can be debated. However, these values are
the consensus of our management and experienced
staff. It is obvious that the Yes alternative,
if chosen, would have higher probabilities of
serious adverse consequences. In fact, we feel
that non-acceptance by EPA and environmentalists
would be almost certain if [this division] were
to agree with the concept of flow variable discharge. We also feel that strong opposition of

one or both of those groups would ultimately
prevent implementation of that alternative.

Based on all of the above rationale (which,
incidentally, is similar to that used by the
City's consultants in their evaluation of the
return flow concept versus keeping existing
discharges in the X and T rivers), it is the
decision of [this division] that the concept of
flow variable discharge to the X River from City
of Y is not acceptable or approvable.

We believe that we understand the City's reasons
for wanting to pursue this matter, and it is our
sincere hope that the City can understand and
agree with [the division's] position. We stand
ready to discuss the matter further with you if
you so desire, and we will provide all possible
assistance in bringing this project to a timely
conclusion.

Yours sincerely,

How radical a departure this letter is from the kind of
rejection that focuses only on the negative aspects of a proposed action. The rejection was presented as the logical conclusion of an evaluation of many factors that were clearly understood by everyone concerned with the decision. Although
the rejection was not entirely palatable to the rejectees, its
objective and thoughtful manner aided in its acceptance with
respect.

Summary

All Yes/No decisions are open to rephrasing and to objective
analysis. The fundamental criticism of the typical Yes/No decision is that it bypasses a careful thinking-through of objectives.
Instead of first considering the purpose of the decision and the
characteristics of a good choice, the decision maker plunges
immediately into an evaluation of *one* of the available alternatives. This often amounts to building a case against that alternative, producing a shortsighted view of the issues. People do
this when they have no other method of evaluating such a
choice. At the same time they may fear that a bad alternative
will slip through unless they make a strong case against it.
When the Decision Analysis procedure is used carefully in this
kind of decision, it is impossible for a truly inadequate or
seriously risky alternative to look better than it is.

Yes or No?
Should We Change or Continue as Before?

Sometimes we must decide either to change a certain operation or continue as before. The decision "Yes, we change" is always accompanied by many unknown factors. On the other hand, the decision "No, we don't change" has obvious flaws—otherwise, the proposal to change would never have been made. However, familiarity with the status quo is a compelling attribute of the No choice.

One of the world's largest insurance companies carried all its accounts and business records in computers located in twelve business regions throughout the United States. Every month these accounts were closed, forwarded to the Central Office, and entered into the central computer to be combined into a single record.

A proposal had been made to eliminate the twelve regional computer records, handle *all* business through a master computer at the Central Office, and downgrade the twelve regional offices to administrative entities. The Executive Committee faced a Yes/No decision: Should the company conduct business in this new way or continue on in the decentralized manner? After debating this issue, the Executive Committee rejected the new method as too risky and complicated.

An assistant to one of the Executive Committee members felt that rejecting the proposal on a Yes/No basis had been inadequate. Although the new method was suspect because it entailed change, there had been no close comparison of the *relative advantages and disadvantages* of the two systems. He asked his boss, a VP, if he could conduct a full-fledged Decision Analysis on the proposal as an exercise in the technique. With grudging permission, the young man began by listing what he thought might be the criteria of an *ideal* insurance accounting system. Next day he took his set of criteria to his VP, explained them, and asked his advice. After they discussed the requirements of such a system, the VP added one item and reworded another. Then the assistant asked, "I wonder how the other Vice Presidents would see these? Would they agree with our list?" His VP took this as a challenge and had the list of objectives circulated among the other Executive Committee members for comment.

When suggestions were received and incorporated, the young man said to his VP, "Some of these are more important than others, but I don't know enough about the insurance business to assign the correct weights." The VP reviewed the list and added weights to the criteria. Again, the assistant raised the question as to how the other members of the Committee would see them. The list was circulated for further comment and approval. As before, suggestions were received and incorporated into the list of criteria.

The assistant took the completed, weighted criteria to experts in both present and proposed systems, gathered relevant data, then submitted this to disinterested managers for an evaluation of the two systems. Their conclusion was that the centralized system would perform *more than twice as well* as the present one against the criteria. On the grounds of "some interesting data I've developed," the assistant requested and received approval for a 15-minute presentation to the Executive Committee.

To prepare for the meeting, the assistant assembled a large chart to display the criteria, some of the supporting information available, and the evaluations that had been made of the two systems against the objectives. One could see at a glance that the proposed system was better on almost all counts. On the day of the presentation, the assistant brought in the experts to answer substantive questions, put up his chart, and explained his findings.

There is much to learn from this example. The Executive Committee had never really framed a decision statement. A sales presentation extolling the virtues of the new centralized system had been made to the Committee by a computer consultant. Most of the discussion that followed was about hardware. No comparison was made with the performance characteristics of the present system. Then the Committee had been asked to make a decision. "Yes, we buy the new system" would imply change and probable headaches; "No" would presume an understanding of the relative performance of the two systems. However, this understanding was impossible without a set of criteria against which "Yes" and "No" could be transformed into distinct alternatives, each with its advantages and disadvantages.

When the young assistant developed these criteria, it made all the difference in the world. A system first seen as too complicated, risky, and troublesome could now be recognized for its real advantages over the old decentralized system.

After two 3-hour meetings during which all aspects of the two systems were discussed and explored, the Executive Committee voted unanimously to overturn its previous rejection of the proposed computer system. The new system was purchased and installed. In the first year of operation, it saved more than $400,000 over the former system. In each year that followed, savings exceeded $500,000. These savings would not have been realized if the two systems had not been compared independently against adequate operational objectives criteria.

"Is It Good Enough?"

In another kind of decision, the question that must be answered is: "Is this proposed alternative good *enough* to adopt?" A current way of doing things is clearly recognized as inadequate. No one is pressing to maintain the status quo. An attractive alternative has been developed or presented, and the people who must make the final decision are almost, but not quite, ready to give it a "Yes."

Executives of a paper and wood products company had to deal with a unique and very difficult situation. Their mill and production facilities were located more than seven hundred miles from their primary market area. Their competitors' mills were much closer, some within the market area itself. This meant that the company was at a disadvantage in cost of distribution and customer service. This disadvantage had been balanced out by lower production costs in their mill area, but that was no longer the case. For the present and the foreseeable future, the higher distribution cost would constitute a major handicap to doing business competitively.

For the past two years the company had worked with a consultant firm, searching for ways to reduce this handicap. An efficient, highly automated distribution system had been designed, based on a set of warehouses within the market area to which unit trainloads of product would be shipped. Now the plan had been completed, with an implementation budget of $11 million. The Chairman of the Board, the President, and all the Senior Vice Presidents had the task of reviewing the proposed system to decide whether or not to accept the consultants' recommendations. Their decision statement was: "Is this proposed distribution system good enough to adopt?"

The group's first step was to set out the criteria of a *perfect* field distribution system—that is, a model that did not appear to be attainable in reality but would incorporate all desirable characteristics. Using this model, the group would be able to judge the quality and performance of the proposed system. Their final set of objectives consisted of six MUSTS and twelve WANTS. All of the WANTS plus only one of the six MUSTS (for brevity's sake) are listed in the chart below. The group assigned weights to the WANTS to reflect degrees of importance; the top weight was 25 rather than the usual 10. The first WANT, "Increase per-share earnings of common stock," was given a weight of 25. Although this objective was not mandatory (therefore not a MUST), its extreme importance warranted its position as a very highly weighted WANT. The other WANTS, listed in declining order of importance, received weights relative to this highest one.

Since their model was a perfect distribution system with optimum performance, each of its objectives was assigned a score of 10. Multiplying each score by the weight produced a weighted total score of 1,120 for the model. The group now had something against which to compare the proposed system. They went through the consultants' plan point by point, evaluating its projected performance against the ideal.

On the first WANT, the plan performed well on four out of five possible ways to "Increase per-share earnings of common stock"; that gave it a score of 8. On the second WANT—"Better, faster service"— the group gave the plan a score of 10. But on the third WANT they hit a snag: They could not justify "Maintain premium sales prices" on the basis of service alone. They would also have to maintain market leadership by having the best quality, most progressive product available in the market area. Since the plan did not provide for a heavy continuing R&D effort, this WANT was scored only 5.

The same thing happened on the next WANT. The company could only "Reduce production costs from present, maintain at lower level" if it spent several million dollars in modernizing the present production equipment. And the plan did not provide for that. The next difficulty was in the ability to "Guarantee continuous supply of product from mill to field warehouses." This too would hinge on modernization of present production equipment.

The complete list, with all scores computed, appears as Figure 10, page 121.

The plan scored only 883 points against an ideal of 1,120, or 79% of perfect. That was not considered to be good enough. Estimates were made of the cost of an R&D effort that would ensure continued product leadership and of the cost of modernizing production equipment. The total went far beyond the MUST of "Total system implementation cost no more than $11 million." Since an improved plan was too expensive, it was ruled out as a NO GO.

But there is a sequel to this story. Having made the weaknesses in the proposal visible, the company and the consultant firm quickly developed a modified plan that would provide money for accelerated R&D and equipment modernization, yet still obtain most of the desired distribution advantages. The modifications raised the total weighted score for the new system to 1,007. This was 90% of the theoretical ideal. The modified plan was accepted and put into effect. It succeeded.

Until the executives of this company had a standard against which to compare their plan, they had no way of knowing if the plan was good enough to accept. Once they developed a model of the perfect distribution system, however, they were able to assess the consultants' proposal and see how close it came to the ideal. This made visible two mammoth weaknesses neither the consultants nor the company personnel had previously recognized. Success of the plan depended on having the best products available in the market area and on maintaining optimum production costs—two factors that had been ignored. If the executives had considered this matter merely as a Yes/No decision, they undoubtedly would have voted in a plan that would have failed entirely or required extensive overruns to keep it alive. It was their clear view of the deficiencies of the proposed system—*as measured against the model*—that triggered the necessary modifications for a successful plan.

Summary

How good is good? A model can be constructed that is so idealistic and visionary that it is useless as a standard against which to judge real-life alternatives. The other extreme is to have too low an aspiration, to create a model no further advanced than the common practice of the day. As in so many aspects of Decision Analysis, informed judgment must enter in heavily. A reasonable model must be constructed, perhaps unattainable in its totality, yet within reach in some of its more important aspects.

There is a caution to attach to the evaluation of "How good is it?" If decision makers settle for an inferior alternative, they block their possibility of finding a better one. A somewhat parallel situation is the medical practice of giving a placebo to a patient. Although the placebo sometimes has a beneficial psychological effect, that patient is unlikely to seek an active medicine that will actually alleviate or cure the sickness. In the same way, a quick and slipshod analysis—ending in the conclusion, "Great idea! Let's buy it!"—is deceptive and dangerous. It has the effect of deluding people into thinking that an inferior decision is better than it really is. Careful analysis, on the other hand, tends to point up weaknesses and show how far from the ideal an alternative is. At the very least, careful analysis provides a realistic platform from which to build improvements and make rational choices.

Figure 10.   Decision Analysis to Determine If a Proposed Distribution System Is Good Enough

OBJECTIVES & CHARACTERISTICS OF AN IDEAL DISTRIBUTION SYSTEM		MODEL		PLAN	
MUST Total system implementation cost no more than $11 million		**GO**		**NO GO**	
WANT	**WEIGHT**	**SCORE**	**WEIGHTED SCORE**	**SCORE**	**WEIGHTED SCORE**
Increase earnings of common stock	25	10	250	8	200
Provide better, faster service than any competitor in the market area	15	10	150	10	150
Justify, maintain premium sales prices	12	10	120	5	60
Reduce production costs from present, maintain at lower level	10	10	100	3	30
Reduce transportation cost, mill to market area	9	10	90	10	90
Guarantee maximum 3-day delivery, any customer in market area	9	10	90	10	90
Maintain complete inventory, full line of products, at minimum cost	8	10	80	9	72
Guarantee continuous supply of products from mill to field warehouses	7	10	70	5	35
Provide truck delivery to all customers	6	10	60	10	60
Maintain minimum costs of handling at warehouses	5	10	50	8	40
Provide modular sealed plastic packaging and handling throughout	4	10	40	10	40
Minimize handling damage to product	2	10	20	8	16
TOTALS **PERCENTAGES**			1,120 100%		883 79%

Florida Power and Light Company's Subdivided Evaluations

In its use of Decision Analysis, Florida Power and Light Company has adapted the "How-good-is-it?" format for use in purchase of equipment, services, and supplies. The company evaluates vendor and product separately, having found that quality in both are requisites for satisfactory performance. The evaluation is divided into sub-parts. For the vendor these include "Commercial considerations," "Technical assistance (capabilities)," "Quality," and "Delivery and storage." Under each heading are a number of performance criteria, totaling twenty-six separate items. Under "Commercial considerations," for instance, the company looks at such criteria as the vendor's financial stability, past performance on claims and adjustments, the completeness of the vendor's bids, and adherence to previous commitments. Each of these sub-parts is given a weight reflecting its importance relative to the other criteria. "Commercial considerations" has a weight of 15% in the overall judgment of the vendor. "Technical assistance" is also worth 15%. "Quality" of service is judged to be three times as important, warranting a weight of 45%. "Delivery and storage" is worth 25%. Based upon Florida Power and Light's past experience with the vendor, each item is scored and the weighted scores are accumulated.

Using a similar process, the company makes a separate evaluation of the vendor's product. Here, the number of sub-parts varies with the item being evaluated. One product, for example, has categories of "Mechanism," "Linkage," "External tank" (a major component), and "Internal tank," with a total of twenty-four specific components or features listed under these headings. As before, weights are assigned and the weighted scores accumulated.

At this point, FP&L moves into a third step: reconciling these evaluations with the price bids made by different vendors. Vendor A, for example, may have a lower price than Vendor B but not provide the same degree of service. The company introduces debits and credits to compensate for the price differences, bringing all values down to a common, equitable comparison. It warns that this procedure does not always result in the contract's going to the lowest bidder, but rather to the vendor offering the best bargain determined by its analysis. This procedure has resulted not only in savings of hundreds of thousands of dollars but in confidence that the company is getting the most for its money. *How good is the contract being proposed to FP&L?* This kind of Decision Analysis has been its best way of finding out. The procedure may not guarantee 100% success in the purchasing-bidding transaction, but it does minimize the possibility of overlooking or misunderstanding factors of potential importance.

Development of an Alternative

Another kind of decision must be made when no ready alternative exists, and the decision maker must decide *how best* to accomplish a purpose. When there is no acceptable known way to do that, this decision-making process starts from zero. The assignment, in short, is "Figure out a way to do X."

"Figure out a way" means that we must select from all available component acts a series of components that will most feasibly and effectively get the job done. To do this we must clearly understand the nature of X—what it is we are trying to accomplish in the first place.

A large sugar company in a tropical country faced a problem for which there was no known solution. Its mills buy cane from local growers and reduce it to crude sugar. The sugar is then exported through a government-controlled consortium at controlled prices. The company buys cane according to its sugar content and sells the crude sugar to the Government at a fixed price. The only way the company can be profitable, therefore, is to produce economically. The crushing season lasts about five months. Early cane has low sugar content and brings less money to the planter. Late cane also brings a lower return. Cane harvested at the peak of the season brings the most money. But not all of the cane that is cut at the peak of the season can be crushed at that time, for the volume available far exceeds the optimum volume of the plant. (This is shown in Figure 11, page 124.) The decision faced by the company was this: Find ways to encourage the delivery of more early and late cane for processing, thereby permitting the plant to operate for a longer period of its optimum level. As indicated in Figure 11, the company's intention was to fill up the hatched areas, representing early and late cane processing. But how could this be done within the limited options of a controlled economy?

The top people in the organization came together to address the situation. Their decision statement was: "Find the best way of ensuring a stable, optimum cane supply to the Santa Elena mill."

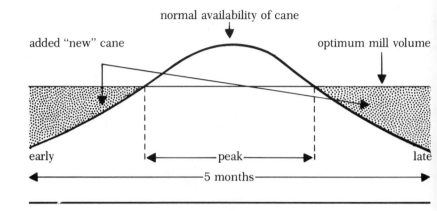

Figure 11.

Sugar Cane Processing

normal availability of cane

added "new" cane

optimum mill volume

early

peak

late

5 months

They then set out criteria that would characterize acceptable actions to encourage or guarantee a stable supply. A good action, for example, would be "legally acceptable" at "lowest cost" with "high probability of success." The team listed these actions as WANTS, and assigned a weight of relative desirability to each one. The complete set of WANTS is shown in Figure 12, pages 126–127.

The team then generated ideas and actions that might ensure a stable cane supply. Some ideas had been talked about for years. Some actions had been used in the past, either by the company or its competitors. Some suggestions were fragments that had been used piecemeal; they were not part of any coordinated plan for dealing with the cane supply.

There were plenty of opinions, but few facts. No one knew for sure what had worked and what had not. About all anyone knew was that the present methods were inadequate and a better way must be found. Now, for the first time, management was going to assemble *systematically* all that was known in order to devise an overall program.

Cane is cut in the field when it reaches peak sugar content, when labor is available, when the weather is good, or when the planter's horoscope and intuition tell him that it's time to cut. Since most planters do not have their own trucks, they must hire trucks and drivers. The roads are very bad, the trucks in terrible mechanical condition, and the loads three or four times the maximum rated weight for the vehicle.

The planter is often a free agent who can sell his cane anywhere. He leaves it up to the truck driver: "Go wherever you can get it and get the best price." At the mill there may be two hundred to three hundred trucks waiting to unload at any time. A truck and driver may stand in line for thirty-six hours before unloading.

The longer the waiting time between cutting and crushing, the lower the cane's sugar content. A delay means less money for the planter.

Some planters have mortgaged their crop to the bank and are obligated to sell their cane to a specific mill. The mill pays the bank, not the planter. To get desperately needed cash, the planter may "polevault"—that is, send a truckload or two to another mill, receive payment himself, and leave the bank wondering why his crop is so small this year.

Because the mill must run at between 95% and 100% of capacity to make a profit, it offers special inducements to planters and drivers. If it loses cane by being outbid by competitors, the mill will run at below the magical 95% mark. If the mill becomes greedy and overloads rickety, poorly-maintained equipment, the machinery may break down, putting the mill out of business. The sugar industry in this tropical country is a cutthroat, brutally competitive affair.

When the team evaluated each of the ideas and actions against the weighted criteria, the results were surprising. The lowest-rated alternatives were kickbacks to drivers and allowing "pole-vaulting" payments to planters—two favorite strategies used by their competitors. The highest-rated idea was to provide a pleasant waiting area for the drivers—a shaded, open-air place for lounging, talking, playing cards, drinking beer, and flirting with pretty waitresses. It would cost little and be enormously successful.

The company owned an underused railroad that wound through the cane plantations. Cane could be loaded from trucks to the railroad cars to achieve stockpiling. This would involve double handling rather than the triple handling of cane off-loaded onto the ground. Free railroad transport to the mill could be tied in as an added incentive. An improvement of the roads leading to the mill was another good idea: it would greatly influence drivers who owned their own rigs and had to pay for breakdowns. Paying a premium price for early and late cane would also help smooth out the production schedule.

Thus, a program was made up of *a combination of feasible, effective choices* that enabled the mill to operate at a much higher level of profitability than ever before.

Summary

The directive "Figure out a way" is often misinterpreted by managers. When they respond by meeting to "get all the ideas out on the table," the procedure is fairly predictable: Lists of alternatives are proposed *even before* all objectives are stated and

Figure 12.

Decision Analysis

"Find the best way of ensuring a stable, optimum cane supply to the Santa Elena mill."

WANTS CRITERION CHARACTERISTICS	WEIGHT
Lowest possible cost	10
Legally acceptable	9
High probability of success	10
Minimum complications of normal operations	7
Minimum risk of overload, plant breakdown	4
Feasible, easy to implement	5
Allows predictable schedules	5
Low risk of interruption by external factors	2
Low risk of retaliation by competitor mills	3
Low risk of offending planters, Government officials	4
Low risk of being cheated	8
Avoids unfavorable precedent, next crushing season	10

ALTERNATIVE ACTIONS

Trucking allowance	Free railroad transportation	Graded, improved access roads	Reduced unloading time	Towing, repair service	Spot cash payment	Advanced payments on contract basis	Guaranteed price regardless of sugar content	Premium price for early, late cane	Profit sharing with planters	Discounts on trucks, parts, fuel and oil	Discounts on tires	Discounts on fertilizer, farm equipment	Kickbacks to drivers	Pleasant waiting area for drivers	Polevault payments to planters
5 / 50	8 / 80	7 / 70	4 / 40	7 / 70	10 / 100	8 / 80	4 / 40	6 / 60	3 / 30	6 / 60	7 / 70	7 / 70	8 / 80	9 / 90	7 / 70
10 / 90	8 / 72	8 / 72	10 / 90	7 / 63	7 / 63	9 / 81	6 / 54	7 / 63	2 / 18	8 / 72	8 / 72	8 / 72	3 / 27	9 / 81	1 / 9
10 / 100	5 / 50	5 / 50	10 / 100	6 / 60	8 / 80	9 / 90	8 / 80	10 / 100	6 / 60	7 / 70	6 / 60	6 / 60	7 / 70	4 / 40	6 / 60
10 / 70	5 / 35	8 / 56	4 / 28	9 / 63	6 / 42	5 / 35	5 / 35	7 / 49	1 / 7	9 / 63	9 / 63	9 / 63	10 / 70	8 / 56	5 / 40
4 / 16	7 / 28	6 / 24	8 / 32	10 / 40	6 / 24	8 / 32	8 / 32	10 / 40	6 / 24	10 / 40	10 / 40	10 / 40	7 / 28	10 / 40	4 / 16
5 / 25	7 / 35	6 / 30	3 / 15	6 / 30	8 / 40	5 / 25	5 / 25	7 / 35	1 / 5	6 / 30	7 / 35	5 / 25	9 / 45	8 / 40	10 / 50
2 / 10	4 / 20	2 / 10	10 / 50	2 / 10	1 / 5	4 / 20	2 / 10	10 / 50	3 / 15	2 / 10	2 / 10	2 / 10	4 / 20	1 / 5	2 / 10
7 / 14	6 / 12	5 / 10	8 / 16	6 / 12	9 / 18	4 / 8	5 / 10	7 / 14	1 / 2	7 / 14	8 / 16	7 / 14	3 / 6	10 / 20	2 / 4
5 / 15	9 / 27	7 / 21	8 / 24	7 / 21	5 / 15	8 / 24	10 / 30	6 / 18	7 / 21	8 / 24	5 / 15	6 / 18	2 / 6	8 / 24	1 / 3
8 / 32	9 / 36	7 / 28	6 / 24	9 / 36	8 / 32	7 / 28	7 / 28	3 / 12	2 / 8	6 / 24	7 / 28	6 / 24	1 / 4	10 / 40	1 / 4
4 / 32	8 / 64	9 / 72	10 / 80	2 / 16	2 / 16	4 / 32	1 / 8	8 / 64	2 / 16	1 / 8	1 / 8	3 / 24	1 / 8	9 / 72	4 / 32
1 / 10	3 / 30	5 / 50	10 / 100	1 / 10	2 / 20	1 / 10	1 / 10	5 / 50	1 / 10	3 / 30	4 / 40	4 / 40	2 / 20	10 / 100	3 / 30
464	489	493	599	431	455	465	362	555	216	445	457	460	384	608	328

clearly defined. As a result, the alternatives may satisfy one or more of the general objectives expressed at the meeting without serving as logical steps to a successful solution.

On the other hand, a group that begins with a well-defined set of objectives has an immediate structure within which it can relate and evaluate ideas. In this context the ideas themselves tend to be of higher quality. The admonition "Don't prejudge ideas or you will stifle creativity" holds true within this format as well. In the case of the sugar mill, the idea of a pleasant waiting area for the drivers was greeted at first with derision. No one had ever heard of such a thing. It was considered trivial. But since it was neither impractical nor irrelevant, this idea fitted very well with the company's criteria.

Working from a set of objectives does not stifle creativity. On the contrary, this format focuses attention on the task at hand and prevents waste of time and energy on suggestions that are clearly irrelevant. It also enables earlier recognition of a good idea. An inadequate basis for evaluation invariably stifles creativity, for it works against the recognition of an excellent idea that may appear to be revolutionary or peculiar.

The Routine Decision

When Decision Analysis is practiced continually and successfully within an organization, its use invariably becomes *required* for certain decisions and *habitual* in choice-making at all levels. The DA habit is very clear in the following example from a large chemical company.

> The company, which produces synthetic fibers, had a standard procedure for dealing with a substandard product. The rejected fiber went into a warehouse, where it stayed until a large quantity had been amassed. The plant manager then would phone his superior at the head office and request permission to dump a few tons of scrap. This gave the head office a control on the amount of substandard material being produced. Permission was automatically granted, the plant manager cleared out his warehouse, and the rejected fiber went to the county dump.
>
> But one day, in the middle of such a phone call, the manager at the head office suddenly asked himself, "What are my objectives? We're supposed to be making money, and dumping tons of fiber like this is crazy!" He refused the requested permission and

told the plant manager to find a non-conflicting market for the fiber that would return some of the revenue to the organization.

The plant manager was shocked. Marketing wasn't his job. He thought he had been given an impossible, unreasonable assignment. But the head office didn't yield. So he made some inquiries and five days later discovered a new market for his synthetic scrap fiber: it was to be cut into short lengths as pile stuffing for sleeping bags. He sold the entire lot for $50,000.

This market for scrap fiber now contributes significantly to the overall revenue of the company. The scrap fiber is used as synthetic pile in ski jackets, coat liners, and a hundred other items besides sleeping bags. Imagine how much potential revenue had been trucked to the city dump in the years before one person asked, "What are my objectives?" and decided that there must be a better way.

Decision Analysis as a Standard Procedure

The requirement to use Decision Analysis for certain kinds of choices is standard operating procedure in many of our client organizations. All that is necessary is that the top management of the organization set the example and set the rules. For example, a number of companies now require that all hiring, transfer, and promotion of employees be conducted according to the Decision Analysis format. This accomplishes many goals. To begin with, everyone is using the same guidelines. All objectives for personnel decisions are clear, visible, and documented.

A Government Agency

What follows is a memo to file written by an executive in a United States Government agency. For all proposals for new hires, the agency requires an accompanying list of objectives for the position to be filled. If the proposal is approved, this list of objectives, or an amended version, will be used as the standard against which candidates will be evaluated.

Everyone who would later be involved in selecting the new planner would have a copy of these objectives or the revised version. And, in this agency, each candidate would also receive a copy before being interviewed.

```
MEMO TO FILE

From:     [Manager]

To:       [Director of Manpower Planning]

Subject: Proposal to Hire Planner for
the _____ Study

Decision Statement: To Select a Planner for
the _____ Study

Objectives                        MUST   WANT / Weight

Minimum 6 months planning
experience                         X

Degree in engineering or
planning                           X

Experience as Study
Director                                  X       10

Registered Engineer or
Planner                                   X        2

Data processing experience                X        5

Available for extensive
work in [city]                            X        8

Can and will work without
guidance                                  X        6

Good communicator at
meetings                                  X        8
```

The L.D. Schreiber Cheese Company

Most routine selections at the L.D. Schreiber Cheese Company, Green Bay, Wisconsin, begin in just the same way. The implementation of a new acid-handling system for the firm's head plant was the final result of a team decision based on these objectives.

```
To:       [Managers Involved]
From:     [Initiating Manager]
Subject:  Objectives of Acid Metering System

Decision Statement:  To Implement an Acid
                     Handling System for Acetic
                     and Lactic Acids
```

MUSTS

1. Machinery capable of handling strong acids
2. Meter directly into cooker
3. Personnel will not handle acids manually
4. System be adaptable with small ($600) changeover cost to batch blending
5. Be usable in existing system

WANTS	WEIGHT
1. System cost under 4,000 to implement	10
2. System to be adaptable as is to batch blending	10
3. Read out quantity on meter that goes into cooker	10
4. Accurate	10
5. Simple to operate	8
6. Simple to maintain	8
7. Similar to present water addition system	8
8. Non-pressurized system	8
9. Push button to actuate	7
10. Digital readout	6
11. Put on line by September 15, 19--	5
12. Use in other plants	4

Once the use of Decision Analysis has become habitual and required, once it becomes "the way we do things here," as it is at L.D. Schreiber, it is a self-perpetuating system.

Florida Power and Light Company

Many routine selection decisions at Florida Power and Light Company are put through a complete Decision Analysis, just to be sure that everything of importance has been considered. One such typical use of the process concerned the selection of a new service yard site in the Miami area.

> Residential expansion in the northwest area of the city during the later 1960s had quickly saturated the capability of the Transmission and Distribution Department, which is responsible for installing and maintaining customer service. Its employees work out of yards where they park the service vehicles and draw supplies and tools. A new yard was needed, but a seemingly "routine

selection decision," once looked at from the perspective of Decision Analysis, showed that the decision would be more difficult than anyone had expected.

To begin with, a utility service site needs space to park many trucks and store bulky equipment and supplies. For a northwest site, an initial MUST objective would concern sufficient space for at least fifty service trucks. Some eighty service personnel might be headquartered at the location. Adding it all up, Florida Power and Light Company needed seven and one-half to ten acres of industrial zoned land in a neighborhood that had become a prime residential area. Utility service yards normally are set up in industrial districts or in outlying areas, where there are few neighbors to react against applications for zoning changes. This surely did not characterize northwest Miami. Suitable and available sites would be few and expensive.

Although the alternatives had a broad range and permitted considerable flexibility, unprecedented expense continued to be a primary factor regardless of which alternative was examined. Transmission and Distribution managers considered all sites that met the primary MUSTS of size and location. Some sites would require draining and clearing of swamp land. Others did not have the right zoning but were considered on the basis of possible rezoning approval.

Eight sites evolved. One site that seemed favorable before Decision Analysis turned out to have long-established industrial zoning—but a bare minimum of usable space. In the same way, the process made visible all the tradeoffs among various alternatives. Ultimately, the Transmission and Distribution team recommended purchase of a $1 million parcel of land. Previous service yards had been built on sites costing no more than $300,000.

How could this very costly alternative have emerged as the best one? With all information visible and plugged into the analysis, one fact became apparent to the managers making the decision: the adverse consequences of failing to establish a successful, suitable facility *with growth potential to meet future probable needs* was the most expensive alternative of all. Florida Power and Light Company had already felt the effects of developing residential areas, overcrowded and inefficient conditions at existing yards, and wasted time and lengthy trips between service locations. Decision Analysis proved the soundness of the "million dollar alternative." The choice was approved on the grounds that thrift today would prove no bargain tomorrow.

Of the thousands of Decision Analyses that have been conducted at Florida Power and Light Company, one, "the computer modernization decision," called for overall expenditures of some $10 million over a five-year period for equipment, system development, reprogramming, and many other requirements. Technical advisors established the performance specifications for the new equipment and its support software and services. In effect, the specifications that evolved became the basis for the analysis. These specifications were included among the objectives for the decision and became "result objectives"—what the decision was ultimately expected to produce for the company.

MUST objectives totaled 30, WANTS 120. FP&L considered that a less comprehensive effort might fail to identify objectives that would turn out to be crucial after the fact. The lengthy analysis was reviewed by operating management and then passed on to the budgetary committee. The committee reached its decision in one week—unprecedented speed for a decision of this magnitude.

Because all the information that was critical to the decision was sorted, classified, sifted, and considered systematically—*and kept visible*—everyone who was affected by the decision and was essential to implementing it was able to quickly review and consider all aspects of the situation.

The technical expertise of the people who conducted this Decision Analysis was not enhanced or altered in any way because they had learned to use the process. *Enhanced skill in gathering and using information* had translated into the ability to fully utilize all technical inputs. It was this ability that expedited this decision and led to its ultimate success.

Adverse Consequences

There is no decision so small, no alternative so obviously excellent by comparison with its rivals, no situation so patently fail-safe that the possibility of potential adverse consequences can be ignored before implementing a choice. If we look for the outstanding time bomb in decision making, *lack of attention to adverse consequences of a choice* is second only to failure to devise a sound decision statement. The examples that follow alert us to this peril.

The One-Trip Commuter Trains

An East Coast commuter railroad wished to improve its service and attract more customers by adding modern, high-speed equipment. Two complete trains of radically new design were obtained from Italy. These low-slung aluminum cars, pulled by special diesel-electric locomotives, were put on the Boston-New York run with a great deal of attendant publicity. They made one trip and were retired, never to be used again.

Something vital had been overlooked. The new trains were low to the rails, but the station platforms along the line were high, built that way to accommodate American-style cars. There was no way for the passengers to get on or off the new super-train. Some tried jumping, and several were hurt when they slipped and fell. In desperation the new train was stopped a quarter-mile outside the stations, and the passengers were invited to walk. Again some people slipped and fell on the rails. The trains, standing on the main line a quarter of a mile outside the stations, blocked the tracks so that other trains were held up.

The fiasco was so embarrassing to the officials of the line that they decided to junk several million dollars worth of rolling stock rather than admit they hadn't asked obvious questions about consequences before ordering the equipment. It was their hope that the error would soon be forgotten. It was. Bankruptcy followed a couple of years later.

In light of the incomplete nature of the information that is usually available for a decision, people will make mistakes. But no one has to make the mistake of ignoring information that can be obtained, or refusing to think about things that experience and imagination tell us may go wrong with a decision.

Buying Orange Crystals

An executive in a food processing company heard about a couple of reclusive old men working in a makeshift laboratory who had developed a method of making superlative orange crystals. (Orange crystals, the ingredients that impart fresh flavor and aroma to an orange cake mix, are difficult to manufacture but they provide the competitive edge between a fair product and an outstanding one.) The executive met with the developers, and the partners agreed to sell small amounts of the orange crystals to the company at a very high price. Sales of the company's orange cake mix went up, and the decision was made to buy the partners out. That was the decision statement, "Buy them out." After much negotiation and payment of an astronomical price, the deal was closed. The food processing company moved some of its people into the ramshackle laboratory, ready to make orange crystals. But it turned out that none of the employees who had remained in the laboratory knew exactly or altogether how to make the crystals. The process was a secret held only by the two old boys. By the time the food processing company found all this out, the secret of the orange crystals had been sold to its competitor for even more money than the company had paid for the laboratory. The sellers had retired to Mexico and could not be reached for comment.

This poor decision may be criticized in two ways. Had the decision statement been worded "Acquire the orange crystal process," the food processing company would have begun by aiming at the product, not at its outer wrappings. But even with the decision statement "Acquire the orange crystal plant" ("Buy them out"), disaster could still have been avoided by asking, "What could go wrong?" *This is what adverse consequence thinking is all about.* Then someone might well have posed the question, "What if we are unable to duplicate the product exactly?" Attention would then have gone back to the process—where it should have been focused in the first place.

Aboard the Chartered Boat

We have said that the adverse consequences of a decision should be examined for probability of occurrence and seriousness should they occur. Depending on circumstances, the meaning of "serious" varies a great deal. Consider its meaning to John in the following example, a case of an adverse consequence with very low probability of occurrence.

> John had been in his government's foreign service for fifteen years. He had done well, receiving promotions as rapidly as the system permitted. When he was stationed in the capital city of a Southeast Asian country, five top officials of the service were scheduled to arrive during the next months. Many meetings and social events were being scheduled for their visit, and John suggested that a luncheon for the visitors be provided at his home.

> John's house was situated on a charming, quiet canal near the heart of this water-bound city. Although the canal was lined with palm trees and masses of bougainvillea, it was not far from the downtown dock of the city's largest, busiest, most heavily used canal. John suggested that the visitors could board a chartered boat at the main dock, see the city's business center from the water, and within ten minutes be transported to the pier in front of his house. After lunch, they could be driven to their afternoon meeting.

> John's boss thought the idea was a great one and told him to make all the arrangements, which he did in meticulous detail. As a part of his arrangements, John chartered a motorboat adequate for ten passengers—the five visitors, John and three of his colleagues, and the driver. The boat was in good condition, and the driver was experienced.

> What could go wrong? Every day the boat carried ten people, trip after trip up and down the canal. Unfortunately, they were rather smaller than the Western government officials who climbed into

the boat to be transported to the luncheon. Fifty yards from the dock, it became exceedingly clear that the boat was about to sink. It did. Everyone aboard could swim, though none had done so in a business suit before, or in any body of water as polluted as this one. All the swimmers made for the nearest dock and were pulled out by patrons of a waterside noodle shop who had been cheering their progress all the way. A larger crowd gathered to watch as the officials were hosed down by the patron of the noodle shop, and everyone on the dock waved gaily while three taxicabs departed with the group for the trip to John's house. There they took proper showers and put on an assortment of items from John's wardrobe while they waited for fresh clothing to be brought to them. Nobody was very hungry.

John's career did not go downhill as a result of this incident. As he put it, "The week after was awful. I wanted to go back to that dock and tie a rock to my foot and jump off. But after about a month, everyone except my boss was laughing about it. I had thought of everything *but* 'What if the boat sinks?'" How probable was it that such a thing would happen? Very probable, once you realize that each Westerner in the boat weighed at least half again as much as the average passenger who rode it every day of the year. So it happened.

Quick and Continuing Use

Quick and continuing use of Decision Analysis pays off handsomely. At every turn, managers should be questioning the recommendations and decisions brought to them: "What are your objectives?" "What are your MUSTS?" "What are your WANTS?" "What adverse consequences have you identified?" "What can you do about them?" By supervising and managing the decision process in this way, managers can have a significant impact on their organizations.

In our experience, most catastrophically bad decisions come about because no one asks such questions. Something obvious is overlooked, usually because no one thinks to look. The initial decision statement is not questioned, so the wrong decision is made. No one thinks to state the MUSTS explicitly, so a laboratory is bought and a much-needed formula is not. It is assumed that there are no adverse consequences worth mentioning, but when it is too late, it is discovered that a devastating one has been missed.

We can make it a habit to ask questions about the *process* followed in making decisions. Twenty times, the questions turn up little. On the twenty-first try, an oversight is discovered that makes it all worthwhile. Face-to-face or over the telephone, in a meeting or in a conversation over lunch, managers should constantly be aware of their obligation to check on the process that produces the decision. It is one of the most important steps in quality control any manager can take. Like the concepts of Decision Analysis themselves, process questions *work*.

Chapter Summary

Decision Analysis provides the decision maker with a basis for saying what is to be preferred on balance with all things considered. Parts of the process may be used in situations that do not require complete analysis. Listing objectives in advance of the need to make a choice can save time and trouble later on. Asking "What could go wrong?" before an action is implemented can prevent major and minor disasters.

The more complex and difficult the decision, the more important it is to take it one step at a time, paying full attention to each of the three elements of the decision-making process: objectives, alternatives, and potential risks. The more intangible and qualitative the data, the more we need to consider individual inputs in making the decision, and the more we need a systematic way of handling information and separate judgments to produce a successful conclusion.

Decision Analysis is intended to be flexible. It is intended to be used in full and in part, to be modified and adapted to meet the unique requirement of each situation. It may be used by an individual, by a casual group, or by a formally constituted task force. It may be used routinely as standard operating procedure for certain kinds of decisions.

Its single greatest advantage for the organization may be that it provides a common language and approach that removes decision making from the realm of personal, idiosyncratic behavior. Some people, to be sure, will always be able to contribute their ideas and communicate their reasoning better than others. Natural ability of this kind varies tremendously. Where a common language is used in a systematic framework for decision making, however, everyone involved will understand *how* to contribute ideas, and everyone will be able to communicate ideas and reasoning. *Team decisions* based on productive individual contributions become a reality.

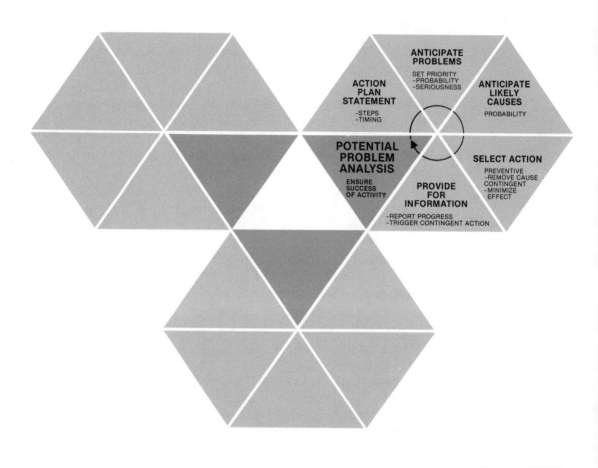

CHAPTER 6

Potential Problem Analysis

Introduction:
Future Events and Their Consequences

Organizations are forever concerned with the future. How an organization will fare in the years ahead will be determined largely by what is being done now, so prudent managers try to look into the future to read the portents they can identify. Yet organizations do not deal with the future as efficiently as they might. Whose responsibility is it to make predictions? And who is to decide what actions are to be taken against speculated but unprovable future demands? Looking into the future remains primarily an individual activity; its results are guided primarily by individual motivation and concern.

It is only when managers share a common method for looking into the future that good things begin to happen. They then have a common basis for sharing and using their expectations. Responsibility can also be shared. Concerns can be identified, the threat they pose can be assessed, and relevant information can be shared for the benefit of the organization. Approached in this fashion, the future offers opportunity, not only uncertainty.

139 POTENTIAL PROBLEM ANALYSIS

Potential Problem Analysis is a procedure that enables us to walk into the future, see what it may hold, and then return to the present to take action now—when it can do the most good. Potential Problem Analysis is the pattern of thinking that enables us to change and improve the future. It is a protective process through which we ensure that the future will be as good as we can make it, rather than allow it to arrive entirely on its own terms. In contrast, Problem Analysis and Decision Analysis are used as they are needed to resolve immediate, visible concerns. The use of Problem and Decision Analysis is demanded by the events of the moment; the use of Potential Problem Analysis is a voluntary act of prudence.

It will come as no surprise that Potential Problem Analysis is used less often and less thoroughly than the other rational processes we have described. It takes determination to make time for deliberating on imponderables and remote possibilities. In fact many of the people who use the techniques of Potential Problem Analysis to protect plans, projects, and operations within their organization have had to learn its value the hard way.

A few years back, one division of a United States paper manufacturing company enjoyed a near monopoly in its most profitable line: fine clay-coated papers for quality color and black-and-white printing. At that time, two-thirds of all the prestige magazines in the United States were printed on this division's papers. Its 90-pound clay-surfaced product was considered unexcelled, and the division was scarcely able to keep up with the demand. If the executives and technical people of the division were somewhat complacent about their success, who could blame them?

Then disaster struck. The United States Congress voted to allow a substantial increase in postal rates on magazines and published materials. Publishers immediately called the paper company and asked for an equivalent paper that would weigh less than half as much per sheet. The division responded by saying that a 40-pound surfaced paper of similar quality could indeed be developed—perhaps within a year's time. The publishers' general response was: "A year's time? Didn't you people ever consider the possibility that this would happen? Thank you, but no thanks."

Within two weeks the division had lost 70% of its business. Customers shifted en masse to a plastic-sized, 40-pound paper that was available immediately from a competitor. It wasn't quite as good as the heavier clay-coated paper, but it was cheaper and cost only one-third as much to send through the mails. And that is what counted most with the customers.

Later, a vice president of the company talked to us about what had happened. "Every element of that disaster was perfectly predictable. We knew our paper was expensive. We knew it was heavy. We knew the Post Office Department had been trying for years to increase third-class rates. But that paper was the golden goose and, as long as it was laying all those golden eggs, there was a sense of security. It would go on forever."

After having lost the major portion of their business, division executives found it difficult to formulate an explanation that would mollify the Board of Directors. The members of the Board held that executives were paid to know whether a situation was loaded or not. And it didn't help to add, "But conditions changed!" Conditions are always changing. Change is what life is all about. Success and survival depend on being able *to anticipate change, and to avoid being swallowed up by its negative effects*. That is what this chapter is all about.

People do not simply ignore the future just because they are busy with the issues of the moment. It is hard to think about the future, to know *how* to think about it. Of course the managers at the paper company might have foreseen a postal rate increase and known its effect on the marketability of their product. Potential Problem Analysis must incorporate such common sense to be useful, but it goes beyond that. Potential Problem Analysis is a systematic *process* for uncovering and dealing with potential problems that are reasonably likely to occur and therefore worthy of attention.

The basic questions we ask in Potential Problem Analysis are: "What could go wrong?" and "What can we do about it *now?*" The specific sub-questions that lead to specific answers constitute the pragmatic and flexible process of Potential Problem Analysis.

Four Basic Activities

The techniques of Potential Problem Analysis are few and easy to understand. The process has been compared to the game of chess: you may learn how to play in a few hours but then spend the next twenty years learning how to play well. For this reason it is not suitable to present a lengthy explanatory example of Potential Problem Analysis in one chapter and examples of its use in the next, as we have done with Problem and Decision Analysis. Instead we will look at the four basic activities that provide the framework for Potential Problem Analysis and then devote the rest of the chapter to illustrating how managers work within this framework to deal with a variety of future-oriented situations.

The four activities are:

- *Identification of vulnerable areas* of an undertaking, project, operation, event, plan, etc.

- *Identification of specific potential problems* within these vulnerable areas that could have sufficient negative effect on the operation to merit taking action now.

- *Identification of the likely causes* of these potential problems and *identification of actions to prevent* them from occurring.

- *Identification of contingent actions* that can be taken if preventive actions fail, or where no preventive action is possible.

The actions that are taken may be large or small, complex or simple. Determination of the kind of actions to take—preventive, contingent, or both—will depend on the subject of the Potential Problem Analysis, economics, feasibility of implementation, and common sense. Every action has a cost, in that it calls for an allocation of resources against some problematic future return. The best bargain, naturally, is high return at minimum cost. A simple preventive action is a good investment when it significantly reduces the likelihood of having to face a serious problem in the future. A complicated, expensive program is a poor investment when it is aimed at preventing a lesser problem that is unlikely to occur.

Even though you may not be an expert in the economics of the paper industry, try to imagine two or three actions that might have been taken to prevent the heavy-paper disaster, or to mitigate its seriousness once it occurred. Then think for a moment about the subject of cost versus benefit received. What actions might have been taken a year or two before the postal increase that (1) would have saved the company from such staggering loss, and (2) would not have been unjustifiably expensive? Would a small developmental project on light-weight papers have made sense? Would research into alternative coatings have been in order? What other kinds of future-oriented actions would have been prudent?

This is as good a place as any to make the point that second-hand Potential Problem Analysis on behalf of other people and their potential problems is always easier and more obvious than Potential Problem Analysis conducted on our own behalf—particularly when other people's potential problems have already become actual ones.

Potential Problem Analysis may sound very similar to the adverse consequence thinking that is done at the end of Decision Analysis, but the two are quite different both in purpose and process. The potential adverse consequences of alternatives compared in a Decision Analysis are *identified* to help us reach a balanced choice: an alternative that fulfills most of our important objectives at minimal risk. In Potential Problem Analysis, by contrast, we are constructing a plan of *action;* we are going to *do* something, perhaps many things, to eliminate or reduce potential problems. There is one point at which adverse consequence thinking and Potential Problem Analysis do touch as natural starting points for action. Managers often conduct a Potential Problem Analysis to protect the implementation of a decision. When they do, any adverse consequences of a selected alternative are addressed in the course of the Potential Problem Analysis.

It is not uncommon for a management team to choose an excellent alternative that has a couple of substantial risks attached to it. They believe "Those are risks that we can PPA. . . ." In other words the risks are real, but they represent potential problems that can be prevented, or whose effects, if they did occur, could be controlled through contingent actions. A few of our client managers require from their subordinates not only a Decision Analysis for all routine selections but a Potential Problem Analysis on the final choice. This may seem like a lot of extra paper work, but in reality it usually amounts to one page appended to the Decision Analysis. This page spells out any potential problems attached to the final choice, and supplies the preventive and contingent actions that have been generated to handle them.

Whatever the details of the situation, the first step in Potential Problem Analysis is to feel concern for the future of some project, situation, or event. This is a matter of attitude and motivation. It is the kind of concern that presses us to begin thinking about potential trouble spots, about our experience in similar situations, and about what we can do to prevent or mitigate problems that have occurred in the past and are likely to occur again. Potential Problem Analysis must begin with a positive posture, a belief that one can and does have a degree of control over the future. One manager said to us: "I have that positive belief that I can change things. I always ask myself, 'Where could we get killed tomorrow?' "

Many people are afraid to look into the future. "Don't go borrowing problems" is an old adage. The message is clear enough. If you look into the dark recesses of the future, you are likely to find trouble lurking there. It is better not to look. Let trouble find you if it must.

By looking ahead with Potential Problem Analysis, you are taking the initiative. The usefulness of the procedure depends entirely upon what it turns up. It is only *after* the fact that we know the value of time spent in Potential Problem Analysis. Perhaps nothing new has been discovered. Perhaps a future problem has been recognized. Either way, the manager who looks ahead is the winner.

Consider the following example of a manager who did look ahead, and how his use of the four basic activities of Potential Problem Analysis affected the event for which he was responsible.

Planning an Inauguration

A new, multimillion-dollar laboratory at a United States Government facility was to be inaugurated within a few weeks. A senior executive at the facility had been designated to manage the inauguration, a highly publicized event with many Washington dignitaries and a few high-ranking officials from other nations as guests. The manager decided to use Potential Problem Analysis to plan, monitor, and protect the success of this one-time event.

Even administered systematically, the inauguration would entail a nightmare of details. It would bring a huge influx of visitors to a facility that had not been designed to accommodate large numbers of people. Because the facility was engaged in scientific work that had received a great deal of publicity, visitors' expectations were sure to be high. A great many things could conceivably go wrong.

Nobody can deal with every possible problem that can occur under such circumstances, and trying to do so is usually counterproductive. Most of us have known managers who unwittingly allow huge problems to develop because the managers are detail oriented without being priority oriented. Where to begin?

Identifying the Vulnerable Areas

The first question this manager asked was: "Where are we *most vulnerable* with respect to success of this inauguration?" What were the vulnerable areas most likely to provide problems that could disorganize, disrupt, or otherwise seriously jeopardize the smooth operation of such an event? He drew on his experience, judgment, and common sense to pose the most likely answers:

a. *Weather:* Rain or high wind could disrupt the proceedings.

b. *Program:* VIPs on the program will not attend.

c. *Facilities:* These will be inadequate to handle the large number of people who turn out.

d. *Confusion:* People will not know where to go or what to do.

e. *Appearance:* The site will be messy, untidy.

The vulnerabilities in this kind of situation all have to do with the failure of plans to be fulfilled. It has been planned, for example, that Senator Cramer, a long-time supporter of the facility and its work, will give the keynote address. If Cramer gives the address, there will be no problem. If the Senator is delayed or absent, the program will suffer. Vulnerabilities are often identified by looking at what has been planned, then thinking of what would hurt the most if the plan were to fall apart.

Another common way to ferret out vulnerable areas in a plan is to approach an upcoming event chronologically—that is, by setting out the steps in the plan. "From right now until the conclusion of the whole event, what must be done?" When the steps have been identified, the vulnerable areas will stand out. *Anything that has never been done before* suggests a vulnerable area. So does *overlapping responsibility or authority* for any activity—a contributor notorious for converting potential problems into real ones. *Tight deadlines* represent vulnerable areas. So do *activities* that must be *carried out at long distance* rather than under direct control of the person responsible for their success.

Weather, the first vulnerable area identified, is something of an anomaly. One does not plan the weather; one can only assume what the weather will most likely be. The entire plan for the inauguration is based upon good weather. What if the weather is bad? (More about weather in a moment.)

No plan ever comes off completely as envisioned. So it can be predicted with 100% confidence that this plan for the inauguration will have its gaps and omissions. Most of these will be annoyances that can be suffered and soon forgotten. But some could be of the never-to-be-forgotten, horror-story variety: "Remember that inauguration out at Botch City?" We all know stories that begin in that way. Identifying the extreme vulnerabilities can prevent a further contribution to the lore. There are not many incidents so damaging that they jeopardize overall success of an entire event, so there are few excuses for failing to search for those that can.

There is a vast difference between setting out the steps in a plan in order to identify vulnerable areas and simply listing things to do. In Potential Problem Analysis, the purposeful identification of vulnerable areas leads to identification of specific potential problems in those areas. This, in turn, leads to specific actions. And this is the vital distinction between intention and process.

Identifying Specific Potential Problems

Identifying specific potential problems involves specifying the WHAT, WHERE, WHEN, and EXTENT of individual things most likely to go wrong within an identified area of vulnerability. The description of the area itself—for example, weather—is too broad and general. What specifically could go wrong concerning weather? Considering the time of year, the inauguration could be threatened by two specific potential problems: thunderstorms and wind. A thunderstorm, with torrential downpour, could occur in late afternoon. Weather statistics gave this a 10% probability—too high to ignore. High winds, with blowing sand and dust, would be less disconcerting. Statistics gave this a lower probability—less than 5%.

Having narrowed the vulnerability of weather down to "late afternoon thunderstorm, 10% probability," the manager had something tangible to work with. He could think about possible actions. He could assess the reasonable threat of thunderstorms to his plans, but to save time he decided that the threat of high winds was too insignificant to concern him further.

The manager's third identified area of vulnerability was "Facilities: These will be inadequate to handle the large number of people who turn out." He turned his attention to two kinds of facilities: those for VIPs and those for the general public. Under each heading he set down a number of specific potential problems. For facilities for the general public, he defined these potential on-site inadequacies:

a. Not enough parking space for cars and tour buses, resulting in serious traffic jams and confusion.

b. Not enough sanitary facilities to accommodate the crowds. Many facilities are within locked, secured areas.

c. No water fountains in the inauguration area.

d. Inadequate seating.

e. Not enough trash cans or garbage containers.

Each of these specific potential problems could be described in detail. Each could be assessed independently: How serious a threat was it to the successful outcome of the event? At the end of a few minutes, the manager had a list of the specific problems that would have to be dealt with in order to protect the success of the inauguration. Now he could begin to think of action.

Identifying Likely Causes and Preventive Actions

Two kinds of actions are available to anyone conducting a Potential Problem Analysis: *preventive* actions and *contingent* actions. The effect of a *preventive* action is to remove, partially or totally, the likely cause of a potential problem. The effect of a *contingent* action is to reduce the impact of a problem that cannot be prevented. Preventive actions, if they can be taken, are obviously more efficient than contingent actions.

The manager searched first for ways to prevent each of the specific potential problems he had identified. What could be done to prevent a thunderstorm? Nothing. But he could prevent a thunderstorm from disrupting the proceedings. Since storms usually occur in late afternoon, he would reschedule the inauguration speeches so that they would be completed shortly after 1 p.m. Tours of the facility could follow the dedication ceremonies. If it rained later in the day, no harm would be done.

Another specific problem was that involving Senator Cramer, the keynote speaker. He might be delayed or cancel out at the last minute; the effect on the program would be devastating. He arranged for one of his staff to call the Senator two weeks, then one week, then two days before the date to make sure that nothing untoward had come up. He had the same person check on the other VIPs scheduled to attend. The purpose was to jog memories and reconfirm invitations. Since control of his guests' priorities and travel plans lay outside his domain, there was little more that he could do to prevent these potential problems.

"Facilities inadequate" did lie within the manager's domain. He arranged to have temporary areas cleared and marked off for extra parking space. Mobile rest rooms were rented from a local contractor. Temporary water fountains were installed, and trash containers were borrowed from other parts of the facility and placed around the inauguration area. Extra seating was arranged. Point by point, he corrected the identified inadequacies.

Most of the entries on his long list of specific potential problems could be countered by simple and inexpensive preventive actions. A typical problem was "Confusion about where to go." The manager had one of his staff people drive onto the facility, pretending never to have been there before. This action enabled him to check traffic signs for clarity and placement. The signs were found to be too few, too small, and too close to turn points to permit a driver to react in time. Large cardboard signs were printed, and the manager arranged to have them placed appropriately on the morning of the inauguration. Other signs, giving times of events on the program, were also prepared and put up. Because these specific potential problems were identified well in advance, a number of preventive actions could be found that virtually eliminated these problems.

Identifying Contingent Actions

Some specific potential problems simply could not be prevented. What if Senator Cramer, in spite of all the phone calls, failed to arrive to give his speech? The manager arranged for a back-up speaker who could step in at the last minute. In fact, he arranged for a back-up activity for every event on the program. He had a canvas roof placed over the speaker's stand for protection in case of an early rain, or for shade if the day was sunny. A reception area was organized in a nearby building should VIPs have to run for cover. No matter what might happen, the show would go on.

Room arrangements were made with a second hotel in the event that VIP reservations went awry at the first hotel or unexpected guests attended. Although additional government vehicles had been requested to prevent transportation problems for VIPs, a few staff members who owned station wagons were organized as an emergency on-call group.

In case the contractor failed to clean the site properly, a Boy Scout troop was enlisted as a last-minute cleanup gang, in return for a promised private tour of the facility later on. The Scouts agreed also to remain on duty, collecting trash, during the ceremony itself. Extra bins and containers were provided to make the task easier.

These contingent actions, designed to minimize the effects of unpreventable problems, would handle situations that were potentially most irritating and troublesome. This would leave the manager and his staff free to deal with other unforeseen problems. They looked forward to the great day with confidence that they had done everything within their power to ensure that the event would run smoothly and professionally. The inauguration would not be marred by disorganization and mistakes.

The Results

It did not rain early. It did not rain late. In fact the weather was so good that the crowd was nearly double the size expected.

Because of a death in his family, Senator Cramer, the keynote speaker, canceled out less than eight hours before the program was to begin. The back-up speaker stepped in as promised. The proceedings went off without a hitch. The extra parking areas, filled almost to capacity, provided enough space for everyone. Traffic moved without incident. Sanitary facilities were adequate in spite of the large crowd. The orderly crowd showed little frustration or confusion. And the Boy Scouts ran in and out, picking up litter, so that the extra trash containers were all utilized.

Until the very last minute of the inauguration, the affair was an exercise in perfection, a model of organization. But it wouldn't be fair to end the story here. Despite the excellence of planning that correctly uncovered most of the problems, people who were there still do say, "Remember that inauguration at Botch City? WOW!"

The Air Force had been invited to provide a flyby as the ceremonies came to an end. And that is what was provided. A transonic flyby. This was in the early days of faster-than-sound flight, and there still were some things to learn. Three jets screamed by at low level, dragging a monstrous sonic boom behind them. More than three hundred windows in the new laboratory were shattered, and a number of concrete support pillars developed instant cracks. The laboratory was opened at 1:30 p.m. and closed at 1:45 p.m.—for nine weeks of repair. There were few injuries, by some miracle all superficial.

Everyone who attended agreed it was the most memorable and exciting inauguration they had ever witnessed.

The moral of this story is that you probably can't win them all, no matter how hard you try. But if you provide a good back-up speaker and enough sanitary facilities, your public will enjoy the show and forgive those rare problems that do drop out of the blue.

There can be no promise or possibility of complete security from surprise. The purpose of Potential Problem Analysis is not to guarantee an error-free future for plans, projects, and events. The cost of such attention would probably exceed its benefits. The purpose of Potential Problem Analysis is rather to reduce the uncertainty of the future to manageable proportions, and to eliminate the kinds of events about which people say too late: "Why didn't somebody think of that?"

A Different Kind of Process

Potential Problem Analysis has one characteristic that makes it essentially different from the rational processes of Problem Analysis and Decision Analysis. Within both Problem Analysis and Decision Analysis, one step leads inexorably to the next, and the steps are followed in orderly and thorough fashion to produce a logical conclusion. That is not always the case in Potential Problem Analysis.

Potential Problem Analysis comprises four logically consecutive steps. However, it is possible to identify potential problems and likely causes for which there are no preventive actions. When that happens we must jump the preventive-action step and go on to devise contingent actions to minimize the effects of the potential problem.

It is also possible to identify serious potential problems for which there are no feasible preventive *or* contingent actions. When that happens, there are only two paths to take: First, we can accept the identified risk and hope for the best. Secondly, we can move back from Potential Problem Analysis into a decision-making mode in order to identify a more manageable course of action.

Our first example of Potential Problem Analysis illustrated all four of its basic activities: identification of vulnerable areas, identification of specific potential problems within those areas, identification of preventive actions, and identification of contingent actions. In the following example, the result of the Potential Problem Analysis process will be quite different.

A Case of Responsibility

If ever an announced decision called for meticulous use of Potential Problem Analysis, this one did. The economic facts of life forced the top management of one of our clients in the chemical industry to order the closing of a facility we will call the Sayers Point Mill. It was obsolete, isolated, too costly to maintain, and located in an area where raw materials were becoming increasingly scarce. Its managers were not surprised at the decision.

However, there was more to consider, much more.

The work force of 984 people from the local area averaged fifty-three years in age. Many had worked for the company for at least twenty years. Educational levels were generally low. Other local job opportunities were nil. Sayers Point Mill managers were faced with the implementation of a decision that was both professionally and personally unpleasant.

It was a situation in which any action would have far-reaching effects. Many of these effects would, in turn, create new problems with their own largely negative effects. For these managers, vulnerability—a key subject in Potential Problem Analysis—included neglect and disregard of corporate responsibility. If we bring change into the lives of others, society holds us responsible for the effects of that change. If we disavow the responsibility, refuse to discharge it, society can bring powerful sanctions against us. In this case the exact nature of that responsibility could only be grasped if management understood exactly what the effects of closing the mill would be.

There could, in fact, be countless effects but no one can deal with all possibilities. Management needed to discover where the greatest specific vulnerabilities lay. Yet it appeared that there would be first, second, and third orders of effects. The managers began by asking, "In what way will this action of closing the mill have the *greatest* impact on us and on others? Where will this action hurt *most*?"

For practical reasons, we will limit ourselves to the top five effects identified by management. The complexity of the situation makes even this partial list complex. To reduce the effects of closing a mill to a few simple terms would be to distort reality.

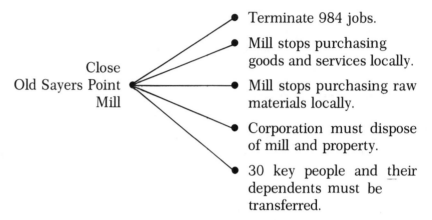

Close
Old Sayers Point
Mill

- Terminate 984 jobs.
- Mill stops purchasing goods and services locally.
- Mill stops purchasing raw materials locally.
- Corporation must dispose of mill and property.
- 30 key people and their dependents must be transferred.

These primary effects are still too general and diffuse to deal with. Before the mill's managers can begin to consider possible actions, they first have to understand the second order of effects. To do this they change the question slightly, asking of each primary effect, "Where will this effect, as a change, have its greatest impact on us or on others? Where are we or others most vulnerable and most likely to suffer because of it?" These questions lead to working out the five or six most important second-order effects:

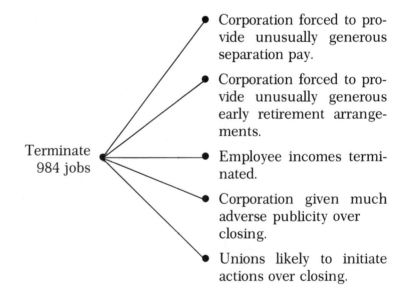

Terminate
984 jobs

- Corporation forced to provide unusually generous separation pay.
- Corporation forced to provide unusually generous early retirement arrangements.
- Employee incomes terminated.
- Corporation given much adverse publicity over closing.
- Unions likely to initiate actions over closing.

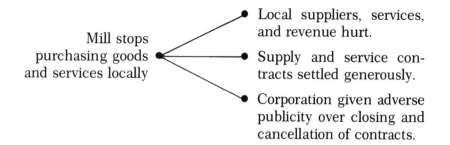

Mill stops purchasing goods and services locally
- Local suppliers, services, and revenue hurt.
- Supply and service contracts settled generously.
- Corporation given adverse publicity over closing and cancellation of contracts.

And so on, through all the first-order effects.

With the second-order effects made visible, the managers now can identify *specific potential problems*. To complete the picture, they need only their past experience and imagination. The results of these changes can be listed as a series of concise statements of outcome:

Heavy cash demands will be placed on the Corporation— on the order of X hundred thousand dollars.

The precedent of unusually generous separation payment for early retirement will cause future trouble.

Many mill employees who are terminated will go on unemployment rolls, some for years to come.

Many will become virtually unemployable.

Local merchants and services will be hurt by reduced purchasing power.

Debt structure of community will have to increase.

Impact on local government will be severe, tax revenue will be reduced, demand on services will increase.

Unemployment will bring social and family disintegration.

Adverse publicity will put Corporation in a bad light, will force it to take a defensive posture.

Closing will create employee distrust and dissatisfaction elsewhere in the Corporation.

Class actions suits will be initiated by unions.

Closing will create union bargaining problems elsewhere.

There will be some local business failures, hard times for many others.

Services and businesses will reduce activity, contribute to numbers of the unemployed.

Suppliers will reduce activity, contribute to numbers of the unemployed.

Suppliers elsewhere will tend to distrust Corporation, demand cancellation clauses more favorable to them.

Precedent of supplier contract settlements will cause future problems.

Damage suits against Corporation may be brought by suppliers.

The managers saw immediately that most of these effects lay beyond their control. These potential problems could not be prevented, for the very nature of the action they were about to take would cause the effects. They could take certain contingent actions. They could provide a large fund for settling claims. They could attempt to transfer more people to other activities. They could phase out the closing over a longer period.

There followed days of heated debate. The company felt it couldn't close the mill, yet couldn't afford to keep it open—and there seemed to be no half-way measure. Then someone suggested that a new process, originally scheduled as a major expansion project for a mill nearly a thousand miles away, might instead be installed in the Sayers Point Mill. There would be disadvantages. There would be some sacrifice in efficiency due to the logistics of the Sayers Point operation. Existing personnel would have to be completely retrained. Totally new equipment would have to be introduced. There would be a host of problems, but solution of these problems lay within control of the organization. By replacing the original plan, "Close Sayers Point," with "Convert Sayers Point to the New Process," all the gut-wrenching effects could be prevented. The decision was made to put the new process into the old mill.

There were some problems in putting the new process into the Sayers Point Mill, but most of the people there responded enthusiastically to the new opportunity. Mill conversion was completed ahead of schedule, and startup of the new process ran decidedly ahead of schedule. The mill achieved full design production capacity before anyone had believed possible and went on to operate at an average of 115% of capacity. The loyalty of the Sayers Point people was totally to the corporation that had taken an action to discharge its responsibility to them.

At the time of writing, the Sayers Point Mill remains the only non-union operation in the organization.

In this case the result of Potential Problem Analysis was recognition of an alternative superior to the one originally proposed. The contingent actions meticulously devised by the management team never had to be used, but the exercise was hardly a waste of time. The process had given them a picture of their situation that was more comprehensive and precise than they could have gained otherwise. There is no better way to see that a decision is a poor one than to examine in detail the probable effects of its implementation. The "walk into the future to see what it may hold" was worth the trip for the managers at Sayers Point and for the company.

When to Use Potential Problem Analysis

When should one use Potential Problem Analysis? Whenever experience and gut feeling say that something could go wrong in the future and the cost of its going wrong could be great for any major project or event, Potential Problem Analysis is essential. NASA, in its space programs, has been a heavy user of Potential Problem Analysis. Dr. Kurt Debus, head of the Cape Kennedy launch complex, told his people, "We can't afford to have *any* problems. We must find them *before* they happen." At every turn he and his people asked: "What could go wrong? What can we do about it now to prevent it?"

Potential Problem Analysis is a technique that enables the manager to make full use of his or her experience. Over the years any manager has seen hundreds of problems crop up that should have been anticipated, and has heard of thousands more. This is the body of experience that Potential Problem Analysis taps and puts to good use. Merely being able to remember a thousand horror stories is of no use unless that body of information can be used to prevent more.

The Likely Emergency

Here is how one manager systematically used his experience and judgment to winnow out the few important and likely potential problems from a host of superficial "maybe problems" in a situation that threatened his organization. Observe how he used his staff to examine and evaluate an uncertain future, and how he used his judgment to set the guidelines. He and his staff were successful precisely because they set tight priorities on the most critical of forecasted problems.

The Managing Director of an overseas branch of a multinational corporation described how he had evacuated his people because street fighting had broken out: "The crisis point arrived suddenly, with scarcely any warning. But we had our evacuation plan ready and everything was rolling in a matter of minutes. Nearly four hundred employees and dependents were involved. We brought them in by private vehicles to a central gathering point, then proceeded in convoy to the airport. Everything went off without a hitch. We sat in the airport until things cooled down twenty-four hours later and then took everyone back to their homes. But if we'd *had* to leave, we could have done so without incident."

"I'd been in that country more than a year before the riots started. I watched the political situation worsen. My experience told me that things could deteriorate overnight and that we could be targets of hostility and violence. I brought my staff together and shared my concern with them. I asked them to consider what would happen if there were a violent overthrow of the government and we had to get out. My greatest concern was how we would protect our people and their dependents. I told my staff: 'Find out where we would be most vulnerable, where events could hurt our people most.' "

"One of the key exposure points they identified was the trip to the airport from the security of our buildings. They showed me an evacuation plan drawn up by my predecessor, with a convoy route clearly marked out. The voice of experience inside me fairly shouted on that one. 'Is it up to date?' I asked them. 'How good is it?' At my urging, a couple of my staff drove the route one noon hour. One of the streets indicated in the plan as safe and quiet, along which the entire convoy was supposed to move, turned out to be a narrow dead end. One bridge they were to use on the way to the airport would have been perfectly adequate—if it had ever been built. Only the approach had been completed. As a result of that analysis, identifying potential problems and correcting them, we had a plan that would work when and if the whistle finally blew."

This manager could very well have asked his people to make a list of *all* the things that could go wrong, writing down potential problems in slavish detail to make sure "we don't miss any." The list would have grown to fearsome length, for hundreds of things could go wrong in such a situation. Some would have been vexatious, some disturbing, some moderately dangerous. But the sheer mass of all the things that could have gone wrong might have obscured the potential few that would have been fatal.

Even more likely, the mass of possibilities would have been so overwhelming that the group would have said, "To hell with it! Let's just wait and see what happens!" That attitude might have led one day to a convoy of the company's employees and dependents being caught in a narrow, dead-end street during a full-scale riot. The manager instead used common sense and good judgment, coupled with his experience, to conduct a systematic Potential Problem Analysis on the few most serious potential problems he and his team could foresee.

Whose Responsibility?

When something has already gone wrong, and it is due to your own actions, you are well aware of whose responsibility it is. But suppose you look ahead and see the potential failure of something for which no one has *direct* responsibility. Whose responsibility is it to raise unpopular questions and suggest possibly needless actions? Unless responsibility has been pinpointed by the organization, your conclusion may be to leave well enough alone.

Serious potential problems are usually broad, affecting many different aspects of an enterprise. It is easy for a manager to say "That's not in my area" and pass responsibility to someone else. Nothing can be more dangerous. A problem that might have been dealt with successfully in its early stages may be difficult or impossible to handle later on. Ideally, organizations should welcome constructive criticism of decisions and policies, but few actually do. This raises a major barrier to effective use of Potential Problem Analysis. Looking ahead and recognizing trouble, then doing something about it, is too often a case of individual managerial courage.

> In the spring of 1966, a Senior Foreign Service Officer assigned to the United States Embassy in Bonn looked into the immediate future and recognized a serious potential problem.
>
> The war in Viet Nam was not going well for the United States, despite major commitment of advisory personnel. The officer felt that President Lyndon Johnson would have to decide within the next two or three weeks whether to escalate that commitment or initiate withdrawal.

Drawing on his knowledge of Johnson's past decisions, he believed that the President would escalate. His scenario included the following. Fifty thousand of our best troops would be sent in. They would be taken from Germany, where they were part of our NATO commitment. President Johnson would give the order suddenly, without full consultation with our NATO partners. This would hurt our alliances, upset the balance of power, create confusion, and erode confidence throughout Europe. Especially in Germany. Our allies would see the replacement troops as untrained and unprepared. Hostile nations would be sure to exploit the situation, and our relations would be badly damaged.

The Foreign Service Officer carried out a Potential Problem Analysis on the situation, listing the major points of vulnerability that occurred to him. He drew some of his colleagues into the study and got additional points of vulnerability from them. They then explored the preventive and contingent actions that might be taken. They created a plan from these elements for dealing with a sudden withdrawal, and alerted others who would be involved. In the end they had enlisted the support of their counterparts in a dozen United States embassies across Europe. The plan of action complete, they waited.

Exactly ten days later President Johnson gave the order for 50,000 troops to be airlifted out of Germany, beginning within twenty-four hours. There was little warning to anyone and no consultation with the other NATO nations. The Officer's prepared plan was brought swiftly into action. Within minutes Foreign Service officers over a quarter of the world were calling on their foreign counterparts, explaining the move, giving assurances, dealing with problems, and answering questions.

There was a minimum of confusion and no appearance of a void in the NATO forces in Europe. By the time hostile nations heard about it, all questions had been answered and there were no embarrassments to exploit. There had been no frantic scramble, no one making contradictory off-the-cuff statements, no duplication or omission, no chaos. It all went off as planned.

The easiest and most economical time to solve a problem is before the problem has a chance to occur. This means that people must feel free to look into the future and suggest actions for improving it, or have the guts to move ahead out of personal dedication and commitment. How easy it would have been for the Foreign Service Officer to have deferred to "those who have official responsibility for things like that!" He didn't. Instead he organized an effort that turned out to be supremely successful and a service to his country. In a quiet way his use of Potential Problem Analysis contributed to changing the course of history for the better.

To the Benefit of Everyone

If the people of an organization care about the future and wish to make it better, and the organization itself is open enough to consider suggestions for improvement, Potential Problem Analysis can contribute to the benefit of everyone. Potential problems are not all of the earthshaking variety. Many uses of Potential Problem Analysis are commonplace. But still, they make a difference. The operation runs more smoothly, there is less waste and confusion, and fewer things have to be done over.

An engineering manager and his chief technician were describing a proposed installation to their boss, head of operations for a major airline. They had designed a quick-service facility to be built in an existing hangar. In the new facility, a jet would be brought in, all seats would be removed and stacked on one side, and a crew would work around the clock on inspections and repairs to have the plane ready to go again in thirty-six hours. Discussion had turned to the storage rack for the seats, a small part of the overall plan. It seemed quite simple, yet the manager of operations said from habit: "What could go wrong? Let's list some things."

A quick Potential Problem Analysis was carried out. The first few items were of no consequence. Then the technician said, "Suppose the deluge system releases accidentally?" The deluge system in an airplane hangar is an oversized version of a commercial sprinkler fire protection system. Modern jets are highly inflammable. They carry huge quantities of fuel and no chance of fire is taken around them. Deluge systems are triggered by sensitive smoke-and-heat sensors and sometimes turn on even when there is no fire. Aircraft workers consider it better to be drenched once in a while than incinerated. But a deluge on two hundred nicely upholstered seats would be another matter. It would put a plane out of commission for days—no trifling concern in a business in which hours of utilization translate directly into return on investment.

What else could go wrong? "We have pigeons in the hangar during the summer." (Something like a deluge system, only smaller.) "What about spray painting?" Overspray drifting onto the upholstery would be catastrophic. Within minutes the original design had been modified to give covered protection to the seats while in storage. Of course the need for coverings for the seats would ultimately have been discovered the hard way. With Potential Problem Analysis the operations manager moved directly to the optimal design.

Potential Problem Analysis is an attitude, an orientation towards the future. It is positive, not negative. It is a way of thinking that says, "We can foresee the future to some extent, and we can change it in some degree to make it better." In a competitive world the balance between success and failure is often narrow. The winning margin is often no more than that gained by foreseeing to some extent, changing in some degree.

Imperial Oil of Canada, a long-time user of Potential Problem Analysis, had an ambitious program of exploration mapped out for the Mackenzie River Delta. The Mackenzie empties into the Beaufort Sea and the Arctic Ocean. As soon as the ice broke up in spring, a task force of ships, planes, and men would converge on the area to search for oil. Their mission would be to set off seismic charges and plot the underlying strata. Several hundred men had been assigned to the project, plans had been worked out in meticulous detail, schedules had been made, and supplies had been dropped and cached along the way. Everything was ready. Then the plan was subjected to a thorough Potential Problem Analysis. "What could go wrong? What negative effects could our actions have?"

At that point the company recognized that vast schools of Beluga, or white whales would be coming into the Mackenzie River Delta for three weeks. There they would have their calves, make new liaisons, and mate before returning to the sea. The Imperial Oil crews would be working in the area at the same time, and the noise and disruption would frighten the Belugas out of their traditional ceremonies of courtship and reproduction. The plans were changed, at substantial cost, and the Delta was left quiet and peaceful. The Belugas arrived, sported in the clear waters, had their progeny and their love affairs, and swam out to sea again, undisturbed.

Chapter Summary

Potential Problem Analysis is, first of all, an orientation, an attitude. It is based on the conviction that one can walk into the future, see what it may hold, then return to the present to take action now—when it can do the most good. Potential Problem Analysis is the pattern of thinking that enables us to change and improve future events. It is a systematic thinking process for uncovering and dealing with potential problems that are reasonably likely to occur and injurious if they do occur.

Potential Problem Analysis asks two basic questions: "What could go wrong? What can we do about it now?" Four basic activities provide the framework for Potential Problem Analysis:

1. Areas of vulnerability are identified: Where could we be most deeply hurt? At what points could change affect us most heavily?

2. Specific potential problems are identified within the areas of greatest vulnerability. These are specific situations that pose so serious a threat that some immediate action is required.

3. Actions are identified that will prevent occurrence of specific potential problems. These actions are directed at the likely cause of the threatening change.

4. Contingent actions are identified that can minimize the effects of potential problems that cannot be totally prevented.

Potential Problem Analysis is not a negative search for trouble. It is a positive search for ways to avoid and lessen trouble that is likely to come in the future. As such, Potential Problem Analysis is one of the most rewarding activities engaged in by a manager or an organizational team. It provides individuals and organizations with their best chance to build the future in accordance with their visions and desires. Potential Problem Analysis is one of the finest tools available for bringing into focus today the best thinking of an informed management team properly concerned with the future.

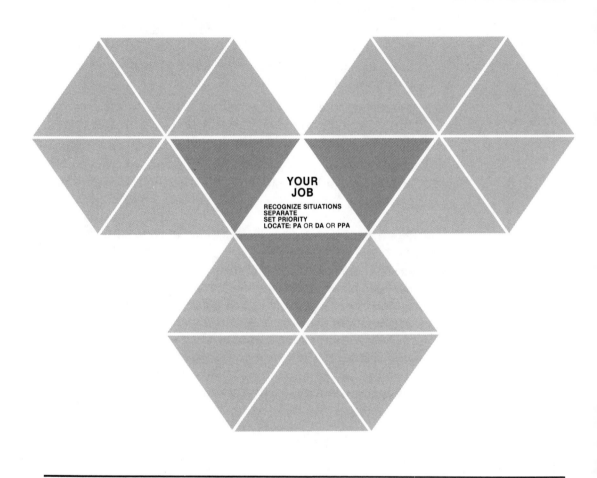

YOUR JOB

RECOGNIZE SITUATIONS
SEPARATE
SET PRIORITY
LOCATE: PA OR DA OR PPA

CHAPTER 7

Situation Appraisal

Introduction:
Situation Appraisal, Tool for Evaluation

In the preceding chapters we have spoken of Problem Analysis, Decision Analysis, and Potential Problem Analysis as discrete processes to be used one at a time, each sufficient unto itself. While this is accurate, the use of the processes from day to day does not consist of a blithe stroll from one to another as circumstances dictate. In actual practice we may experience confusion and uncertainty over where to begin, how to recognize situations that require action, how to break apart overlapping and confusing issues into manageable components, how to set priorities, and how to manage a number of simultaneous activities efficiently.

Nearly every manager has entertained the fantasy of starting fresh. Fantasy indeed. Even on the first day in a new job, the manager is beset by issues that were chronic frustrations for the previous incumbent. Lying in wait for the new manager, in addition, are new issues, problems to be solved, and decisions to be made. All these are part of the job. They do not stand on ceremony. They move right in. Before the week is out, potential problems begin to suggest themselves. The opportunity to start fresh does not exist. Every manager must

163   SITUATION APPRAISAL

operate from a middle ground, surrounded by the accumulated problems of the past, a profusion of demands of the moment, and the certainty that future threats and opportunities await him and must not be ignored.

The three rational processes we have already described consist of *analytical techniques*. Their purpose is to resolve situations and issues. Situation Appraisal, by contrast, consists of *evaluative techniques* that lead to proper selection and use of analytical techniques. This process builds the framework for daily use of rational-process ideas. It enables managers to make best possible use of the techniques of Problem Analysis, Decision Analysis, and Potential Problem Analysis by showing them

- Where to begin

- How to recognize situations that require action

- How to break apart overlapping and confusing issues

- How to set priorities

- How to manage a number of simultaneous activities efficiently

A manager skilled in the three basic rational processes works more efficiently than an unskilled one in handling information about specific problems, decisions, and potential problems. To be effective in the overall job of managing the daily disorderly flow of information, however, a manager must also be skilled in the process we call Situation Appraisal. Managers lacking this skill cannot make frequent or productive use of the analytical rational processes, because they are uncertain of how, when, or to what end the processes can be used. These managers tend to await the arrival of ready-made problems, decisions, and future-oriented concerns that fit the techniques they have learned. When that doesn't happen, they become frustrated. The situations that actually do land on their desks are invariably confused, multifaceted, overlapping, and fragmentary. As a result the managers fail to recognize the situations as subjects for Problem Analysis, Decision Analysis, or Potential Problem Analysis. Frustration sets in, and the managers are apt to say, "I thought those ideas were great when I learned them, but I haven't used them nearly as much as I thought I would. . . ."

There is nothing wrong with spontaneous use of individual rational processes. But the degree to which they are used on a continuing, systematic basis depends on the degree and frequency with which the manager uses the evaluative management techniques that are about to be presented.

Situation Appraisal Techniques

Situation Appraisal techniques enable the manager to increase competence in these four activities:

- Recognizing concerns
- Separating concerns into manageable components
- Setting priorities
- Planning resolution of concerns

Figure 13.   **The Stages of Situation Appraisal**

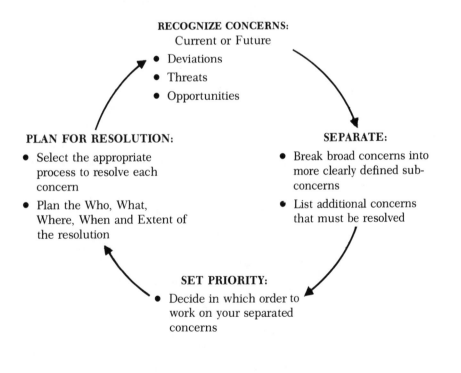

RECOGNIZE CONCERNS:
Current or Future
- Deviations
- Threats
- Opportunities

PLAN FOR RESOLUTION:
- Select the appropriate process to resolve each concern
- Plan the Who, What, Where, When and Extent of the resolution

SEPARATE:
- Break broad concerns into more clearly defined sub-concerns
- List additional concerns that must be resolved

SET PRIORITY:
- Decide in which order to work on your separated concerns

These four stages do not form a lockstep sequence. If we had all the information about every concern, as soon as we recognized it, and no new concerns came up until we had resolved all of those on our list, this would be the logical sequence to follow. In reality, however, new information is constantly coming to light. No sooner do we start the analysis of our highest priority specific concern, than someone rushes in to tell us that the problem has been solved or that someone has discovered that it is really two or three smaller problems. When this happens, a new list of concerns must be made, more separating questions asked, priorities reset. Each situation may demand a different order and combination of Situation Appraisal techniques.

The basic techniques for each activity are described below. Following the descriptions are examples of the techniques in practice to show how skillful managers use the techniques under everyday conditions.

Recognizing Concerns

A *concern* is any situation that requires action and for which you have full or partial responsibility. In other words, something needs to be done and you are in a position to do something about it.

Where do these concerns come from? Sometimes both the source and the mandate for action are very clear. Your boss has given you a specific task. A routine report is due at the end of the month. A subordinate's performance has become unsatisfactory. A project you are heading is not going to meet its deadline.

Such concerns are straightforward: something needs to be done and you are the person who has to do it. But the most efficient managers do not spend their days responding only to obvious mandates. They search out situations that require action and for which they can take some degree of responsibility. They do this not because they have time on their hands and enjoy troubleshooting for its own sake, but because they have no time to waste on troublesome situations that need never have occurred.

We realize that surveying your job environment for all the concerns that require action is no small task. Many managers have found that it helps to break the search into four activities:

1. List current deviations, threats, and opportunities

2. Review progress against your goals

3. Look ahead for surprises (within your organization and in the external environment)

4. Search for improvement

At times you will want to go through all four activities —at an annual planning session, for example. At other times it will be more appropriate to limit yourself to one or two of them (for example, to plan your week's work on Monday morning, you would only go through the first activity; reviewing progress against goals might happen monthly).

In some organizations Situation Appraisal techniques serve as an outline for routine meetings, helping to coordinate the team's resources and efforts to resolve important matters. Each kind of issue is considered in turn: chronic situations, inadequately handled situations, and unexplored situations.

In the initial step of Situation Appraisal, we identify concerns by asking specific questions:

*   Where are we not meeting standards?

*   What problems from the last six months remain unsolved?

*   What recommendations are we currently working on or will be coming up in the near future?

*   What decisions need to be made now?

*   What decisions are being made now and will have to be implemented when a choice is made?

*   What major projects, systems, or plans are about to be implemented?

These questions are jumping-off points for discussion. Their eventual product will be a list of problems, decisions, and future-oriented concerns that deserve consideration.

When a manager uses Situation Appraisal on an individual basis, this step may consist only of a mental review of current concerns. He or she may also jot down a few notes or list the concerns. But whether one manager is making a quick mental tally, or a team of managers is citing concerns that someone lists on an easel at the head of a conference room, the process is about the same. By beginning this way, we move toward eventual identification and assignment of concerns that can be resolved through partial or full use of one of the three analytical rational processes. At this point, we make no identification of which analytical process applies. Before we can make identifications, we must examine each concern to determine whether it is in fact a single concern or a composite of two or more concerns. If it is a composite, we must isolate and examine each concern on its own merits. Once we have made all these determinations, the next step is to arrange the complete list of concerns in a realistic and useful order of priority.

Separating Concerns into Manageable Components

A combination of *concerns* presenting themselves as one *situation* cannot be dealt with effectively. We must assume that all issues and concerns that have earned our attention are more complex than they first appear to be. This assumption is usually correct. But even if the concern turns out to be simple, our exploratory process, to examine whether it should be broken down, is still useful. This exploratory process ensures that we take the steps of information-gathering necessary for evaluation of all concerns, simple or complex. At the same time the status of a concern will be understood in the same way by everyone involved in its evaluation and eventual resolution. It is unlikely that time will be wasted by employing the separation step of Situation Appraisal.

We asked questions in the initial, recognition stage of the process in order to identify situations that require action. We now ask more questions in order to break apart any situation that consists of two or more components:

- Do we think one action will really resolve this concern?

- Are we talking about one thing or several things?

- Are we in agreement as to the reason we are concerned about this?

- What evidence do we have that says this is a concern?

- What do we mean by. . . ?

- What is actually happening in this situation? Anything else?

- What do we see (hear, feel, smell, taste) that tells us we must take action?

- What is there about the way we handled this situation that should be improved?

- What is really troubling us about this situation?

Like the recognizing questions, these separating questions are jumping-off points for thinking about and discussing our concerns. Some of the questions may seem to overlap, but each represents a slightly different angle for viewing a concern. Taken together these questions get beneath the superficial description of a situation to elicit hard data. They shift the emphasis from opinion to verifiable information.

It is while attempting to separate concerns that the individual manager may pick up the phone to check out facts or verify assumptions. When a team is using these separating questions, we often find that two or three people discover that they have different information, therefore different viewpoints, about the same situation. Without separating questions it is entirely possible for people to sit through a meeting in the mistaken certainty that their individual, disparate assessments of a situation represent the understanding of the group at large.

It is always useful to spend the little time it takes to ensure that a concern that appears to be singular is really singular and that the concern is understood in the same way by everyone participating in its evaluation and eventual resolution.

Setting Priorities

Only after we have separated complex concerns into their components can we set useful, sensible priorities. In the expanded list of concerns that results from separation, each discrete issue we extract from undifferentiated "basket concerns" can be seen to have its own unique features and claims to priority. For example, a concern is originally phrased "Need to hire additional account managers in the Midwestern and Western regions." It is subsequently separated into its components: "Need to hire additional account managers in the Midwestern region" and "Need to hire additional account managers in the Western region." Now we may see whether the priority of one may be significantly different from the priority of the other. This is an important point because it represents one of the recurring pitfalls of priority setting. Concerns must be broken down into their component parts in order to set sensible priorities.

We must also have an organized, systematic way of determining what those priorities ought to be. As managers we may agree on the wisdom of organized, systematic setting of priorities, but in practice this activity remains frustrating and difficult for a great many of us.

"What is the most important thing to do first?" is not a useful question. When you ask ten managers to define "important," you learn why. One will laugh and say, "My boss said do *that*. . . so *that* is most important!" Another will think about it for a while and then say, "The situation that will have the most serious impact on operations if you *don't* deal with it—that's the most important, the one you deal with first." Both answers are fair enough in their way, since they represent disparate but perfectly valid objectives.

A practical and systematic process for determining importance is to consider each concern in terms of the three dimensions listed below. This process can be used in any situation, against any content, by an individual or by a group in pursuit of a common goal:

- How *serious* is the current impact of the concern on productivity, people, and/or resources?

- How much *time urgency* does it have?

- What is the best estimate of its *probable growth*?

On the basis of one or all of these dimensions, we can judge that one concern is *relatively* more important than another and should therefore be considered first. Or we can judge that one concern is *relatively* less important and should be considered later.

When a manager works alone to set priorities, the concerns are usually limited enough in number to be bounced off one another rather quickly in terms of these three dimensions. But when the task is carried out by a team, based on an extensive list of concerns, the first thing that needs to be done is this: *They must cut away the concerns that rank low in all three dimensions, and designate them for further consideration at an appropriate time in the future.*

A typical large-scale use of Situation Appraisal occurs when a team of managers is considering a great many issues. In such a case it is essential for the team to expose the few *critical concerns*. It is within this critical minority that the team must initially determine the relative priorities. When twenty-five concerns have emerged following separation, we do *not* ask, "How do all the concerns stand, each compared with the others, on the basis of their relative seriousness, time urgency, and probable future growth?" This process would be a gigantic waste of time. Anyone who tried to do such a thing would have no time left to resolve any of the twenty-five concerns.

Any experienced managerial team making an orderly evaluation of all twenty-five concerns can pick out, let us say, the top five in a relatively short time. Discussion of the three dimensions of seriousness, time urgency, and probable growth would then be confined to relative assessment of those five critical concerns. This does not mean that the other twenty concerns disappear. They are simply set aside until an appropriate future time. Nothing is missed, nothing lost, but no time is wasted working on concerns that today are of low priority in all three dimensions. They may be dealt with safely next week or next month.

Why does the setting of priorities seem so straightforward when we read about it, and become so difficult when we try to do it? Managers usually do an unsatisfactory job of setting priorities because they approach each issue as it comes along, on the merits of its isolated apparent importance. Even if they sense that priorities should be set on the basis of relative criteria, it doesn't seem to work out that way in practice. Internal rules for determining what is important are very gradually developed over a long period of time. We work on one concern even though we *know* that we should be working on something else that may have more serious effects, that may be more urgent, or that appears to be getting out of hand. Why do we do it?

Because of our backgrounds, abilities, and technical expertise, each of us has certain *kinds* of concerns that give off high-priority signals regardless of their relative fit in our daily roster of concerns. Management activities *we enjoy most* make stronger bids for our attention than they may deserve. Concerns that reflect the demands of *demanding people* carry weight that may be totally out of proportion to their importance. They assume high priority because of the nuisance content inherent in not giving them precedence. Everyone's ability to set and abide by reasonable, rational priorities is eroded by these and many other natural human factors.

In the midst of so many demands on our time, it requires real discipline to set priorities on the basis of relative seriousness of impact, time urgency, and probable growth. It requires even more discipline to abide by these priorities, given the eroding influence of the many issues around us. But the results are worth the discipline. Nothing brings home the wisdom of setting rational priorities better than the effects of its absence: *What is more obvious than the order in which things should have been done?*

Planning Resolution of Concerns

During the three steps of recognizing, separating, and setting of priorities, we focused on *what* needs to be dealt with. In this step of Situation Appraisal—planning the resolution of concerns—we focus on *how* these concerns may best be resolved, who will handle them, and the *kinds* of answers we need.

In the recognition step we asked questions that would isolate situations of concern that reflect the three aspects of managerial life: accumulation of past concerns, demands of the moment, and future threats and opportunities. In the separation step we clarified these concerns, breaking them down into components as necessary. In setting priorities we focused on concerns that had the greatest seriousness of impact, time urgency, and probable growth viewed from the perspective of the overall number of situations requiring action.

Of these remaining high-priority concerns, some are easy to identify as subjects for partial or full Problem Analysis, Decision Analysis, or Potential Problem Analysis. But it is not always so cut and dried. To ensure that we choose the correct technique or combination of techniques, we must answer a few questions about the *kind* of answer that is required for each of these concerns:

- Does the situation require explanation? Is there a deviation between expected and actual performance? Is the deviation of unknown cause? Would knowing the true cause help us take more effective action? If there is a deviation *and* it is of unknown cause, we can use the techniques of *Problem Analysis.*

- Does a choice have to be made? Or do objectives need to be set in order to undertake some activity? If so, we can use the techniques of *Decision Analysis.*

- Has a decision been made but not yet implemented, and is it necessary to act now to avoid possible future trouble?

Does a plan need to be made to safeguard some decision or future activity? If so, we can use the techniques of *Potential Problem Analysis.*

The *kind* of answer we need determines the choice of rational process. *How much* of an answer we need determines whether we will use all of a process or only part of it. We may, for example, understand the cause of superior performance in one sales district of a manufacturing company. Yet it may be useful to draw up a specification, comparing the superior district with all others. In this way we may gain a more precise understanding of the factors that set that district apart. This situation requires only a partial use of Problem Analysis.

The partial use of Decision Analysis is extremely common. Suppose that the need to hire a manager for a new position has been identified as a high-priority concern. At this time, weeks before candidates have been selected for interview, the company sets precise objectives for the new position. Later, when candidates are available for interview, those objectives will be ready to use as criteria in the selection process. This sequence provides time for review and refinement of objectives by those most concerned with the new position and with the new manager, as well as the impact of both on the operation. It is far more efficient to undertake this partial use of Decision Analysis early in the hiring process than to postpone full-scale Decision Analysis until the need to make a choice has become imminent.

Partial use of Potential Problem Analysis techniques is called for when it is suspected that a competitor may be about to launch a new product. Full use of the process, complete with preventive and contingent actions, may amount to overkill in response to a faint rumor. In the event that the possibility becomes a probability, however, a review of potential problems becomes a useful step to take. If or when it seems worthwhile to complete the process, the groundwork will already have been laid, and all necessary information will be available.

What is important is that we have identified and initiated specific rational-process techniques that are relevant to resolution of concerns. The point is not to divide concerns among three boxes for subsequent full application of Problem Analysis, Decision Analysis, or Potential Problem Analysis. The point is to use those *ideas* from each that are most suitable and time-efficient for doing the jobs that need to be done.

Once we have identified the techniques we will use to

resolve each concern, we may well have the ultimate in TO DO lists! We will have recognized the situations that require action, broken them down into components as necessary, established priorities, and identified the techniques we will use to resolve them.

The usefulness of Situation Appraisal, however, does not rest entirely on making all information visible. More often than not, the greatest individual benefits of the process accrue from the simple habit of putting on the brakes as soon as things seem to be happening too quickly. *First* you consciously adhere to the discipline of recognizing concerns. *Then* you separate the concerns into manageable components. *Then* you set priorities. *Finally* you plan for resolution of concerns that have the highest relative priority.

When Situation Appraisal is a team activity, the next logical steps are delegation of concerns to be resolved, establishment of time frames for their resolution, and determination of periodic review points.

At the conclusion of a formal Situation Appraisal session, or of any meeting in which the techniques are used as an outline for coordinated discussion of concerns, the end result is that people leave with vital information. They know what situations of concern exist, and what individual components make up these concerns. They know what the priority concerns are and why. They know what their own specific responsibilities will be. They know exactly what techniques they are going to use to attempt to resolve the concerns that have been delegated to them. They know the kinds of questions they need to ask to get started. They know how much time is considered adequate for the tasks they have been assigned. They know how and when to report their progress. They will get the greatest possible benefit from their use of the analytical rational processes, because they have participated in the best possible use of the evaluative rational process.

Situation Appraisal in Practice

Knowing everything one needs to know about a process is of little use if the process is not put to use. The following discussion illustrates how some managers have used Situation Appraisal.

Life in the Middle Ground

We have said that every manager occupies a middle ground within the accumulated concerns of the past, the demands of the moment, and the problems of the future. Let us see how one manager used the techniques of Situation Appraisal to deal with Pandora's box of complex and overlapping concerns.

A complaint reached the manager of the data processing department for one of the largest banks in the United States: "Sue's reports are late again!" Along with the complaint came a cryptic suggestion: "Put some pressure on. We're getting tired of this."

"I asked Sue a few questions," said the manager. "She agreed that her reports were late, and increasingly so. So we began to break down the situation, going through all the kinds of reports for which she was responsible. That's when I found out that information for a certain one of our customers was nearly always late in getting to her. The delay in turn slowed up her output across the board. Now we were looking at a problem that was slightly different from the one presented to me."

Did Sue know why this information was slow?

"Sure, because of the high number of errors in that account, which involved a great number of transactions each week."

Why so many errors in that account?

"That was the next interesting discovery. She didn't know and felt it was none of her business, even though those errors were damaging her own reputation on the job."

What happened next?

"I dropped the 'Sue's reports are late again' problem to investigate the problems in that one account. My assistant and I called on everyone involved. We found twenty-seven separate concerns, including unclear instructions, equipment that couldn't read all the mark-sensing digits, and interference in the optical reader from a black border printed around the customer's checks. Each had to be dealt with on its own merits, and we had to set priorities on their resolution very carefully. Some concerns had to be resolved before others could be understood well enough to work on. A few were self-explanatory but two problems required full use of Problem Analysis over a period of two weeks before they were understood. Several required Decision Analysis, or at least parts of the process. We did a lot of objective-setting in order to come up with better procedures for some of the tasks on that account. If I had accepted the initial complaint, reacted immediately, and done what was asked—'Put some pressure on'—the situation would have been twice as bad in another month."

Today's complaint is often the last visible effect in a long chain of cause-and-effect events. When we use Situation Appraisal and ask specific questions, we can identify actions that appropriately address each of the many conditions that lead to that final visible link.

Stop and Think

It sounds obvious, even elementary to say that anyone who is going to deal effectively with a complex situation must stop and think, not strike out immediately to set things right.

But people are inclined to want to do something decisive and dramatic. "Don't just stand there, *do* something!" expresses a mode of action that sounds better than it works. People also tend to panic, as the manager in the following example might well have done—but didn't.

> One of our clients manufactures cardboard containers for high-quality food packaging. One day, the sales manager received an urgent call from an angry customer, drove immediately to the customer's plant to investigate the complaint first-hand, and walked right into a blast of invective.
>
> "Your cartons are no damn good!" came first out of the customer's mouth. "We're through doing business with you as of right now. My lines are held up because your cartons are bent and mashed. I've got three rush deliveries I can't make, and those customers have been on our phones yelling all morning. Get your truck over here and take this junk back!"
>
> Is that enough to ruin a person's day? The sales manager counted to ten, took a deep breath, and began mentally to separate the the concern:
>
> 1. The customer is frustrated and mad. He's dumping a lot of emotion because there's nobody else around who will listen to him or give him any real help.
>
> 2. He needs some good cartons as soon as possible to get those rush deliveries out.
>
> 3. He's losing money and reputation, and needs assurance he'll be protected.
>
> 4. Something's wrong with those cartons and the cause has to be found quickly.
>
> 5. Whatever's causing the trouble must be corrected to the customer's satisfaction so that it doesn't happen again—or it's goodbye, contract.
>
> 6. If the cause of the mashed cartons is in our plant, this is only the beginning of a major problem.

The sales manager told the customer he understood how serious the situation was and promised to straighten it out to the customer's satisfaction as quickly as possible. He got on the phone and got another truckload of carefully inspected cartons on the way—rush. He got clearance from his head office to cover the customer's losses if the cartons really were at fault. He reported these actions to the customer to assure him that something useful was being done.

Then the sales manager began to ask questions about the nature of the damage: what it looked like, where it had first been recognized, when it first had appeared, and so on. He learned that there had been no trouble until that very morning, and he knew that no other customer had reported any problems with the same carton.

He asked the customer whether there had been any change in material handling in his plant. Yes, as a matter of fact they were using a new side-gripping forklift out on the loading dock.

The sales manager and his customer got to the dock just as the replacement cartons arrived. They saw that the lifters on the forklift were out of line for handling the pallets on which the cartons were stacked. The lifters were mashing some of the cartons in unloading. The customer was satisfied that the cause of his trouble had been identified and that it lay in his own shop, not with the container company. The forklift was adjusted and further damage was avoided. No cancellation of business, no return of goods. The sales manager and the customer parted good friends, the customer somewhat sheepishly affirming that he had received excellent service.

The sales manager stopped the action by entering into it. He took the situation apart, broke it into components, and sorted it out. He identified six major concerns: customer frustration and anger, need for good cartons, need for protection against loss, need to find the cause of the damage, need to correct the problem to the customer's satisfaction, and need to ensure that the problem was not affecting other customers.

He quickly assigned priorities: first get good cartons to the customer, then assure him that he's protected, then find out what's causing the trouble and how to correct it. He decided what kinds of questions he needed to ask for each of the six sub-concerns *before* he set to work to resolve the overall concern.

He had saved himself and everyone else a lot of time and trouble by taking a little time to think through the situation. Imagine what might have happened instead if he had set out to find the cause of crushed cartons being sent out from his plant, or if he had stayed in his office while he dispatched an immediate replacement into the destructive arms of the new forklift on his customer's dock.

A Difference of Opinion

Confusion about the nature of a situation is always a giveaway that separation or more separation is imperative before the situation can be dealt with effectively. That is why, during the separation step, we ask whether there is disagreement over the cause or the nature of each situation under discussion. We want to avoid, for example, getting all the way to the point of specifying a deviation, only to find that there is a considerable difference of opinion as to exactly what information belongs in the specification. The following case demonstrates how such separation can lead us toward resolution.

> A team of technical people at a tire company was attempting to specify what had been termed The Sidewall Separation Problem. Rubber had separated from tire sidewalls during use, and now they were trying to find out why.
>
> "But it's also on the foot of the tire," one person said. "To my knowledge, it isn't," countered someone else. Rather than wrangle over differences, two specifications were begun—one on the sidewall, the other on the foot.
>
> "It isn't separation of rubber *that has adhered*. It is failure to adhere properly in the first place," someone offered by way of clarification. "Not so!" was the immediate rejoinder. "It's torn away from the sidewall!" Non-adherence was a new factor, so it became a third deviation to be specified.
>
> It became obvious within twenty minutes that the reason the sidewall separation problem had never been explained was that three separate deviations, each with its own distinct cause, had been woven together. Separated and individually described, the three deviations began to make sense. The introduction of a new, fast-acting solvent was correlated with the non-adherence complaints—a cause that was checked out and confirmed the next day. The other two deviations were explained within the week. None of the three deviations had been open to explanation as long as they remained locked together.

This example points out the usefulness of thinking through a situation before taking action. But if this team knew how to use Problem Analysis, why didn't they also know how and when to use the techniques of Situation Appraisal?

"We never even thought of it," said one member of the team. "We felt that this was one problem, and there was considerable pressure to get it resolved quickly. We didn't stop to think that people on the team might have differences of opinion as to what the problem actually consisted of, much less that we were dealing with three separate problems. Since then we have made it standard procedure to go quickly through separating questions at the outset of any discussion about a problem. Facts, evidence, effects, disagreements, actions already taken. All those questions. It only takes about five minutes and it's worth it. It is not all that uncommon to hear more than one version of the same problem. I'd say, in fact, that the sidewall separation problem was fairly typical."

What Kind of Action Makes the Most Sense?

In the fourth step of Situation Appraisal, we make judgments of the kinds of actions that should be taken to resolve high-priority concerns. The questions we ask lead to partial or full use of Problem Analysis, Decision Analysis, or Potential Problem Analysis. It is important to remember that two equally critical factors must be considered in making this judgment: *the nature of the concern* and *the kind of answer that is required.*

The personnel people first learned about The Madge Problem when her supervisor came to them and said that Madge was upset and unable to work. Why? She felt that people were staring at her. This was so disturbing that she "couldn't stand it anymore." A visit to her workspace showed her to be no more exposed to public view than any of the other ten people in her section. What to do?

Was this a matter to be explained? Should Problem Analysis be used? Not by anyone in the office, in the opinion of the personnel specialist. A psychological cause was likely, one beyond the competence of anyone in the organization (and certainly beyond any legal right of inquiry). Madge had been a good employee. Until the staring problem, she had never given anyone cause for concern. Could some positive adaptive action be taken? Yes, easily. File cabinets were rearranged to give her more privacy. Feeling less visible, she was happy. The personnel specialist went on to other matters, matters requiring more time and effort than the moving of a few file cabinets.

Not all problem situations demand a precise explanation. Another example of a problem that *does* represent a deviation between expected and actual performance but does *not* require a search for cause in order to take appropriate action would be another rise in the price of oil. *Why* the rise is irrelevant for most of us, however irritating the fact may be. The questions that do matter for us are: "What do we do now? What choices do we have? What actions can we take?" In problem situations such as this, the sensible question is not "Why did this happen?" but "What can I do?"

It is also true that there are times when Decision Analysis techniques are not required in order to make a decision. A drive motor has just overloaded and burned out. Cause is known: an operator misused it out of ignorance. The only action to take is replace the motor with one that will work. No Decision Analysis or part thereof is needed. As for Potential Problem Analysis, that's another matter—Preventive Action has to be taken so that burnout doesn't happen again.

Nearly every action has implications for the future. These implications should be explored. After using Potential Problem Analysis, you may find that there are no serious threats around the corner. This certainly is important for the manager to know. However, if something new is recognized, you are forewarned and forearmed. You have an opportunity to take control of the situation rather than have it dictate to you.

It is a rare manager indeed who uses Potential Problem Analysis to the point of overkill. On the other hand, our experience tells us it is extremely unwise to assume that everything has been fixed up once and for all by the most recent corrective action or the most recent decision. Just because Problem Analysis or Decision Analysis has been used skillfully to resolve a high-priority concern does not mean that nothing bad will ever happen again.

Two basic functions are served when focusing on a given situation. First, you clarify in your own mind where you are going. This enables you to allocate your time and energy most efficiently. Secondly, you know immediately the kinds of questions you need to ask, the kinds of information you need to gather. Everyone reading this book has sat in meetings where the discussion went round and round—now touching on why something happened last week, then on what to expect next, then on what to do about it this week, then back to speculations on the something that happened last week. This type of meandering may be expected when people have no pattern to follow, no process for gathering, handling, and directing information toward specific purposes.

Once you have determined that you need to know *why* something has happened, you know that you are concerned for the present only with questions that will lead you to cause. These will be Problem Analysis questions: WHAT, WHERE, WHEN, and EXTENT, to begin with. All other kinds of questions, speculations, and general commentary should come later, in proper place and time.

If the answer you require is *which* alternative should be chosen, or *which* course of action adopted, then you are concerned for the present only with questions that will lead to a balanced choice: What are the objectives for the decision? Which are MUSTS? Which are WANTS? What alternatives are available? And so on through the Decision Analysis line of questioning.

If the concern represents some possible future threat, then you need to discover what specific potential problems exist and you need to identify actions that can be taken in the present to avoid or minimize future trouble. The questioning will focus entirely on the nature of any potential problems, and on the preventive and contingent actions that can be established to preclude them or lessen their effects should they occur. Only Potential Problem Analysis questions will be used as long as this future-oriented concern is being addressed.

When a team of managers agrees that this is the most efficient and productive way to handle the concerns for which it is jointly responsible, everyone—using the same process—respects and contributes to the line of questioning that suits the subject at hand. It is a far more efficient and productive way to proceed than the usual *ad hoc* approach. This is how one executive in a pharmaceutical company put it: "Some of our groups use a rational-process format for their meetings, some don't. The difference between the approaches is clear. When I walk into a meeting where people are discussing something in that format, I can tell within a very short time where they've been so far and where they're going next. I do not need a twenty-minute rehash of the meeting in order to figure out what's going on."

A Situation Appraisal Case Study

Sometimes a forbiddingly complex situation that has resisted efforts for months or years becomes the subject of Situation Appraisal as a last resort. This is what happened in a mining company located in the Philippines.

This open-pit mine depended upon a great many vital pieces of equipment that were obsolete, badly worn, and in need of replacement. Yet the company's top managers, 350 miles away in Manila, had failed repeatedly to appreciate this situation. They had never produced a long-term plan for equipment updating. Because the company recently had embarked on an extremely and increasingly expensive new mineral development in another location, corporate attention was focused on the new venture. What was desired of the old open-pit operation was a minimum number of problems and an uninterrupted flow of profits. This defined which pieces of equipment had top priority for replacement: those which, if lost, would directly interrupt the generation of revenue.

The operational people at the mine felt that their backs were up against a wall. A formal Situation Appraisal session was convened. Its purpose was to address the overall concern of "convincing top management in Manila to set up a program for phasing out and replacing equipment that was obsolete and no longer economical."

This "basket concern" was separated into three components:

1.   What equipment are we talking about?

2.   Why hasn't this problem been solved before?

3.   What does the head office really want from this mine?

Priorities were established. The top-priority question was the second: "Why hasn't this (to us overwhelmingly obvious and important) problem been solved before?" What *had* gone wrong with previous requests? Why didn't top management see the situation the way we did? Since cause was unknown, this called for a Problem Analysis. In short order several causes were developed:

1.   Top management had never been given any coherent, overall picture of the situation that could have led to appreciation of its true importance.

2.   Top management had always been given *lists* of complaints, but never a sound *plan* for replacement of specific equipment in a specific sequence. Managers at the mine had waited instead for corporate personnel to turn the lists into a plan and then act. This expectation, it was decided, had not been realistic.

3.   A documented cost justification specific to the units to be replaced had never been presented to management.

4.   No credible Potential Problem Analysis had ever been presented to management to show the predictable costs of *not* instituting an equipment replacement program.

Put differently, no comprehensive recommendation for specific action had ever gone to Manila. As a result, the real and serious issues the mine faced might well be interpreted in Manila as a collection of ill-defined and endless complaints—an assumption that was subsequently verified.

Priority number two: "What does the head office really want from this mine?" led to a discussion of the needs and objectives of the corporation. The subject of the new mineral development was discussed fully. Top management clearly was not going to be deflected from that project to react in any major way to the plight of the old mine—unless that plight were presented in an organized, accurate, and credible report. The report not only would have to describe the mine's problem but also offer a sound, persuasive, organized plan for meeting its needs.

Through a Decision Analysis, it was decided that a written report of the situation at the mine should be drawn up immediately. This report would contain the following:

- A thorough Potential Problem Analysis concerning present vital equipment, indicating the effect of breakdown on productivity, profit generation, and administrative attention.

- A proposal for establishing standards and measures of obsolescence.

- A listing of equipment to be replaced, with order and priority of replacement indicated.

- A plan and schedule for orderly replacement of equipment, including lead times, production requirements, labor, and other pertinent factors.

- Documented cost justification for each piece or type of equipment to be replaced.

- A Potential Problem Analysis of the proposed replacement plan, with actions indicated to ensure that it would be carried out as stated.

The report was forwarded to Manila. Top management gave it plenty of attention. While they did not agree to every single element of the plan, and not all recommendations were accepted, a positive, orderly phase-out and replacement policy was established.

The mine's managers did not get everything they wanted, but they did get what they wanted most. In a situation in which operating managers had felt powerless, a way of achieving progress had been found. Little or no progress could have been made until they were willing to give up their old definition of the situation—"Top management will not support us"—and replace it with the factual, specific, separated components of the situation. Phrasing the components as questions helped them to clarify the situation further. Priorities were set. They then compiled factual answers to *why* the problem hadn't been solved before, *what* the head office really wanted from the mine, and *what* equipment was of concern. The answers, as you have seen, were not entirely palatable in that they pointed directly to deficiencies in the mine managers' previous handling of the situation. But they also pointed to productive actions that could be taken to resolve the situation. These actions produced the top-management response sought unsuccessfully for so long.

Chapter Summary

Far too much time and effort are wasted in trying to make sense of concerns that actually are unruly *collections* of concerns, each with its own unique features and requirements. Far too many unproductive actions are taken as a result of poorly set priorities and lack of attention to the kinds of answers required by individual management situations.

The use of Situation Appraisal techniques can significantly cut down the amount of time and energy wasted on misunderstanding and misuse of information. These techniques can help managers take more productive actions more often by setting priorities rationally and paying precise attention to appropriate answers. Finally, these techniques enable managers to make best possible use of the analytical rational processes on a continuing and systematic basis, which is the key to their greatest payoff.

Situation Appraisal is the starting point for any effective team action. For how can a team of well-intentioned people function if they have not reached agreement about where they are going and which concern to deal with first? Using Situation Appraisal techniques welds a diffuse group of people into a concerted team, with the efforts of all its members focused in a common cause. It brings together the best thinking of all its members and organizes their actions so there is a minimum of duplication and misunderstanding, and there is maximum effectiveness in dealing with priority matters.

Situation Appraisal is getting ready to do something, the preparation of a rational point of departure. The results of the evaluative techniques of Situation Appraisal are enhanced understanding of management concerns and accurate identification of time-efficient, appropriate actions for resolving those concerns. Such results can bring the manager and his people as close to starting fresh each day as reality permits.

CHAPTER 8

Managing Human Performance Problems

Introduction:
A Real Challenge for the Manager

Sooner or later, in talking about daily concerns, a manager will say something like this: "What really gives me trouble are *people problems*." Pressed further the manager defines people problems in terms of performance: *people do not do what is expected of them*. Since the manager's job is to accomplish company goals through and with people, resolution of human performance problems is a key to success.

The objective of this chapter is to demonstrate the application of Rational Process (Problem Analysis, Decision Analysis, and Potential Problem Analysis) to human performance problems. In 1979 Kepner-Tregoe acquired the Praxis Corporation, a specialist in a rational approach for improving human performance systems within an organization. The Performance Analysis Process developed by Praxis complements the approach we discuss in this chapter.

It is one thing to try to find out why an oil filter leaks, why a paint sprayer clogs up, or why a chemical process unit underproduces. It is another thing to search for the cause of a valued employee's poor or declining performance, and yet another to define appropriate corrective action.

A piece of equipment has no self-esteem, but the kind of person you want working for you has plenty. Identifying the shortcomings of a machine or a system can have only a positive effect on future performance. Not so with people! You can successfully use rational process techniques to investigate and resolve a wide variety of human performance problems, but you will need far more deftness in questioning, flexibility in approach, and plain tact than you will ever need in handling a hardware problem.

The full process of Problem Analysis is as appropriate for human performance problems as it is for all other kinds of problems. *Problem Analysis is a systematic method for understanding the true nature, and therefore the true cause, of off-standard performance.* In hardware problems the usual result is the selection of an appropriate *corrective* action to remove or successfully work around the true cause. In human performance problems the usual result is *adaptive* action, aimed at adapting to or modifying the impact of the cause.

During an analysis of unacceptable human performance, there rarely is a "Eureka!" discovery of one difference or change that leads to cause. Cause nearly always points to the work environment, not to the person. Sometimes the cause is complex, involving matters that are private to the individual and beyond the expertise or responsibility of the manager.

In dealing with a human performance problem, then, experienced managers know that identification of a reasonable adaptive action is both a sensible and attractive expectation. The reasonable adaptive action improves the situation and avoids the painful, sometimes destructive confrontation no manager likes to think about. Is this taking the easy way out? Hardly. It is the manager's job to get things done. Making adjustments in someone's job and relationships is often the best way to help that person become more productive.

Decision Analysis is deeply involved with the successful management of human performance problems. The cause of the problem may lie in the past, but it is what lies *ahead* that concerns the manager: the best use of the individual's strengths and resources to accomplish the goals of the organization. The better the choice between available alternatives, the better the result for all concerned.

Potential Problem Analysis also contributes to the management of human performance problems in the sense that giving a person a fair chance to perform well is an important aspect of handling human performance problems. If the manager anticipates job difficulties and takes actions now to prevent or minimize them, those actions may spell the difference between success and failure in working with people. Much of what is implied in the phrase "consideration for others" is embraced in Potential Problem Analysis. With both Decision Analysis and Potential Problem Analysis, present action results in fewer problems in the future.

It is inaccurate to speak of "solving people problems." It is far more to the point to discuss "managing human performance problems." In everyday management we seldom explore the many ways that exist to deal with human performance problems. Too often we prefer to coast along in the hope that the problem will magically go away.

The most creative and humane way to deal with people lies elsewhere: We must *manage* a human performance situation, perhaps by adjusting the environment to arrive at the best resolution both for the individual and the organization.

The Most Common Human Performance Problems

We once asked a number of managers to give us "the first example of a typical human performance problem that comes to your mind." As you would expect we received quite an array of responses, some bearing the brush marks of bitter experience. These were the most common themes:

> A new employee, who is supposed to be just great, is a complete disappointment.

> A person who once performed well no longer does—at least not all of the time or on all aspects of the job.

> Performance in one whole department declines steadily over a period of months. There is no obvious reason for the decline.

> There is continuing repetition of needless errors.

> An employee is antagonistic.

> An employee is unwilling to take responsibility.

An employee insists on taking more responsibility than is appropriate.

An employee is frequently absent/late.

Employees play politics instead of doing the job.

The workers have a poor attitude.

We will explore most of these themes in this chapter. All lend themselves to various Problem Analysis, Decision Analysis, or Potential Problem Analysis techniques. All imply some performance ACTUAL that is below a stated or understood SHOULD. In each case some choice of action must be made. Since the management of human performance begins in the past, continues through the present, and extends into the future, Potential Problem Analysis will be appropriate in some form.

Manage or Solve

To manage or to solve human performance problems is not an either-or choice. We would like to resolve such problems insofar as we can. At the very least, we want to be able to manage them effectively. Within the body of Problem Analysis, Decision Analysis, and Potential Problem Analysis techniques, we can find a number of contributions to the management of performance problems—and therefore to the management of human resources in general. These techniques help us to understand cause-and-effect relationships. They set guidelines for making important choices. They provide a mechanism for anticipating and avoiding future trouble. And they provide techniques for breaking down complex and intertangled matters into simple and manageable elements.

Trying to Answer "Why Did It Happen?"

Defining and Communicating a SHOULD

If a performance SHOULD is to be achieved, it must be clearly communicated to and fully understood by the person who is to perform. A surprising number of apparent performance problems vanish overnight when a manager merely defines and communicates the SHOULD to the person whose performance has been unacceptable. People cannot be expected to meet standards that have not been explained fully.

Describing the Problem Situation

When a problem situation is made visible, we can begin to see the difference between fact and opinion, between reality and speculation. This visibility is brought about by a factual, comparative specification in the four dimensions of Identity, Location, Timing, and Magnitude. This process requires disciplined questioning and gives us a basis for challenging information that may be biased or untrue. It helps us sort out individual concerns and break apart the unwieldy lumps of information that typify most human performance problems. A tight specification provides the basis for a fair hearing for the individual, regardless of what the situation may be.

In Chapter Two we presented the questions to be used in specifying a problem. In the use of Problem Analysis in human performance problems, the questions are similar except for some of the wording. The earlier UNIT and MALFUNCTION now become WHO/WHAT and BEHAVIOR OBSERVED. We will also see that there is greater flexibility in the specifying questions as they are used for performance problems.

Specifying Questions for Human Performance Problems

IDENTITY:	WHO is the person (or group) about whose behavior we are concerned?
	WHAT, *specifically*, is that behavior? (Include actions and remarks made by the individual.)
LOCATION:	WHERE is the behavior observed?
TIMING:	WHEN did this behavior first become apparent? and WHEN since that time did we observe this behavior?(If there is a recognizable pattern in the timing of the behavior's occurrence, note it.)

MAGNITUDE: What is the EXTENT of the behavior? (For example: How many complaints? How great an effect on the operation? How widespread the effect of this behavior?)

The goal of these questions is a full-dimensional view of the situation. This includes *everything seen and heard* that answers a specifying question and appears to have a bearing on the situation. Any speculations that must be made for a time along the way should be acknowledged as such ("temporary and speculative") until they can be checked out, verified, or discarded.

On the other side of the specification—the areas of close logical comparison in the problem's four dimensions—we follow exactly the same procedure we follow in the hardware variety of Problem Analysis. We want to know about the person who *could* be exhibiting the undesirable behavior, but *is not;* the task that *might* be performed poorly, but *is not;* and so on throughout our specification. We will then have a comparative analysis on which to build our subsequent evaluation of the total problem.

The following human performance problem, which we have adapted from a real-life situation, illustrates how this process works. It concerns the high error rate of Bob, accounts payable clerk in a small manufacturing company.

> "Bob is not motivated to do the job" is the deviation statement (and heartfelt opinion) of the manager. He is fed up with Bob's performance. Although motivation may eventually turn out to be a factor in this situation, the term really provides very little information at this point. "Bob IS unmotivated, but others ARE NOT unmotivated."

What do you do with that? We need *facts* in order to construct either a deviation statement or a specification; opinions and negative feelings are not enough. What is really behind the manager's negative feelings? Two questions often help a manager spring out of this deadlock of frustration: "WHAT specifically makes you say that?" and "WHAT do you mean by that?"

"Why do you say Bob is unmotivated to do the job?"

"Because he obviously doesn't give a damn. He has been able to do error-free work, but now he's content to turn in a sloppy job and average three percent errors."

"What exactly do you mean by 'error-free work'?"

"Before I brought him into my shop six months ago, he worked in Marketing at the same kind of job and didn't make any errors. And he filled in for Jim, handling expense accounts, and didn't make any errors at all."

Now we begin to get somewhere. We rarely find someone whose performance is poor across the board. Some aspects of performance are bound to be acceptable or even excellent. There is nearly always a considerable range. If Bob's performance had been totally unacceptable in every conceivable aspect of the job, the manager would have fired him long ago and would not now be carrying out a Problem Analysis. But it is sometimes tough to enumerate those parts of the job that are *not* a problem. There is a tendency to ignore what is going well and concentrate only on what is going badly. That, after all, is what needs to be explained. But if the situation merits analysis, then it deserves all the explicitness and objectivity we can give it. To accomplish this, we ask questions designed to get *behind* the feelings, to get to the facts that have produced them.

In specifying human performance problems, comparative information is particularly important because it provides us with insights that may otherwise be unobtainable. If a person does well on one part of a job but not on another, there must be a reason. Whatever the reason may be, comparative information is essential. You develop it from the answers to IS and IS NOT questions: WHO/WHAT? WHERE? WHEN? EXTENT?

"Bob, accounts payable, IS making too many errors; Jim, expense accounts, and Betty, accounts receivable, ARE NOT making errors."

"Bob IS making errors now; WAS NOT for over a year when he worked in Marketing."

"Bob DOES make errors on comptometer work, accounts payable; DOES NOT make any errors at all on other work, as when he filled in for Jim on expense accounts."

Identification of DIFFERENCES from the Specification

As managers we provide an analytical approach that focuses on the *total* environment when we identify *all* components of a situation: the sharp factual contrast between the performance of one person and another, or between one task and another for the same person, or between performance in one work place and in another. This approach is far more efficient and significant than one that settles on an individual's shortcomings, as though he or she were isolated from everyone and everything else. Something is obviously different about that one part compared with the other.

What is the implication of such a difference? Does the person lack skill for one part of the job and not for the other? Are the expectations and instructions clearer for one than for the other? Are conditions for doing all parts of the job equally favorable? Does the person have feelings about one part that get in the way of good performance? If you ask such specific questions, perhaps the person can tell you. Perhaps the person isn't even aware that there *are* differences. Your pointing them out may unlock new information for everyone. Perhaps you can only interpret the differences by drawing in other information from your own experience and from the experience of others.

When you have discovered a body of IS and IS NOT information about a performance problem, you have struck paydirt. IS and IS NOT facts seldom appear as coincidence alone. *Bob is making too many errors. Jim and Betty, on relatively similar work, are not.* This rules out factors common to the three employees and points us toward Bob and his unique characteristics. He is younger than the other two, has more education, is ambitious and aggressive. *He is making errors now but wasn't while in Marketing*—which was also accounts payable work. But he did other things besides accounts payable and he worked with another kind of machine. For Bob, coming to his present position was a change to a more mechanical, less varied job. *He makes errors on the comptometer, but not on what little other work comes his way*—as when he filled in for Jim.

DIFFERENCES Characterized by CHANGE

When we identify changes in the work environment, we are providing more than just clues to the cause of current difficulties. Once we recognize that a specific change produces negative behavior or a decline in performance, we can use this information to improve the implementation of similar kinds of changes in the future.

Generation of POSSIBLE CAUSES

Differences, changes, and tight specification suggest possible causes. All causes we generate from these sources emerge from known facts about the problem situation in all its dimensions. They do *not* emerge from speculation about the person's behavior. A tight specification also helps us use our experience as managers. We can tap the insight and understanding we have gained from years of working with people and dealing with other performance problems.

We saw before that Bob makes errors on comptometer work but not on other work. What is different about comptometer work compared with the other work Bob is doing? What does this suggest as a possible cause? Bob is *bored out of his mind, punching the comptometer all day long.* He's young, ambitious, and aggressive. Perhaps he's being underutilized in his present spot. His strengths—as they appear on the IS NOT side of the specification—are that he is cooperative and a good worker (although not accurate with the comptometer), and does a fine job on expense accounts, as he did on his other work in Marketing.

TESTING of Possible Causes

We must remember that bias and guesswork are with us during every work day. A manager may be convinced that the true cause of John's slipshod performance on Project B is that "he's just plain lazy." But if John worked day and night on Project A, and turned in an outstanding report, and this fact is reflected in the specification ("Deviation IS poor performance on Project B. . .could be but IS NOT poor performance on Project A"), then "just plain lazy" simply will not survive the test against the facts. That possible cause cannot convincingly support and explain all the facts recorded on *both* sides of the comparative specification.

VERIFICATION of Most Probable Cause

When we formally verify a problem's most probable cause, we are protecting everyone concerned. Without verification we may be tempted to build a case for a particular theory about somone's unacceptable performance. Every bit of evidence seems to fit perfectly, and a lax test of the cause does not give enough grounds for rejection. Only upon verification of the possible cause, when additional confirming information is gathered, does it become apparent that the theory is wrong.

> Bob's manager had him in for a chat. Bob said he liked his job but didn't feel much enthusiasm for it. He said he'd enjoyed the expense account work that he'd done while Jim was away. He was sorry about his error rate and said he'd try to do better. Bob improved slightly in the days that followed but, as the manager could now see, Bob's heart just wasn't in it.

> A month or so later Bob was assigned Jim's job on expense accounts. Jim was promoted to a job he had wanted for some time. The new arrangement worked out extremely well. Much later Bob said he was glad to be rid of the comptometer. Asked why he hadn't said something about it earlier, he replied that he hadn't any other choices open to him. He had wanted to keep his job until something better turned up—either with his present employer or somewhere else.

Was the problem solved or managed? It doesn't make much difference. When specific questions were asked, information became available. This information resulted in actions. The actions improved the situation for everyone. The whole matter began with the manager claiming that Bob was unmotivated; it ended with the department retaining a good worker in a job he really liked and performed well. In another case, asking the same questions might have turned up a fault in equipment, inadequate working instructions, or some other true cause. Here the fault lay in job placement of the person.

In another case, an underwriter in an insurance company was accused of slipshod work, low productivity, and a negative attitude toward her job. Everything fitted that cause *until* the assumed cause was verified. The company found that the underwriter had a case load nearly 50% heavier than had been supposed. Neither she nor her superiors were aware of the discrepancy. The case load was adjusted and the problem disappeared. As this case illustrates, managers dealing with performance problems have an obligation to take particular pains in the verification of the most probable cause. It is too easy and too human to see only those facts that fit a preconceived but incorrect theory.

Verification of a problem's most probable cause as the true cause serves another vital function: it provides documentation in support of a personnel action. It is important to have visible evidence of the entire process by which a performance problem was evaluated. It is equally important to have on file the reasons for the final conclusion about cause, and a record of subsequent actions. When an employee is dismissed on the basis of a verified cause, many managers file a copy of the related Problem Analysis and subsequent Decision Analysis for use in the event of a challenge of the dismissal. This kind of record has been accepted as legal evidence in courts of law of the factual, objective analysis carried out in arriving at the decision to dismiss.

Hunch and intuition enter into the analysis of human performance problems. All of us have years of experience in dealing with other people, and it is important that we make full use of this wealth of information. It is a priceless resource, bought and paid for the hard way. During careful Problem Analysis we can tap that resource in the most productive manner.

Our research into the management of performance problems tells us that most errors come about as a result of *lack of solid data* rather than through misinterpretation of the data, and as a result of reliance on rumor and supposition. Given enough solid information, most managers can draw on their experience to good effect. Given fragmentary information or unfounded speculation about a person's motives, the same managers are likely to commit an error.

The key to successful management of human performance problems lies in the *quality* of available information. Problem Analysis, Decision Analysis, and—as we shall see— Potential Problem Analysis demand disciplined, systematic collection and organization of data, reliance on fact, and constant challenge of information of unknown quality. In every problem situation these procedures for handling and visibly arranging data can only improve our use of experience to interpret information and give it meaning. Intuition and native judgment work best from a base of good information.

Deciding What to Do

Setting Clear Performance Objectives

In managing human performance problems, we must set clear objectives because of the danger that bias and emotion may enter in, perhaps unconsciously, to sway our judgments. Objectives state *explicitly,* in visible terms, what we are trying to do. They provide a valuable check on our motivations. In addition they are useful in communicating our positions to other people. Objectives can be commonly understood by a group of people, so the sharing of information and experience becomes more efficient. This is important in managing human performance problems.

Setting clear objectives is also vital in matters of personnel selection and performance evaluation. In personnel selection, objectives form a visible set of criteria against which a choice will be made. They provide all candidates with the fairest possible basis for consideration. In performance evaluation, objectives form a visible set of measures against which an assessment can be made. Objectives constitute the SHOULD for the employee—a set of guidelines against which to model his or her own performance. Setting clear objectives takes the mystery out of working with others, and ensures the possibility of satisfactory performance.

Nobody likes to fire anyone. Moreover, by the time a manager decides to fire someone, the investment in that person may already be sizable. There is a certain loss of face, not to mention money, when we have recruited, hired, trained, and managed a subordinate over a period of time and then have to admit we were wrong: "He just didn't work out the way I hoped." "She doesn't seem to be right for the job." One attribute effective managers share and respect is the ability to find, effectively manage, and keep the best people.

One of the best ways to avoid having to fire people is to give everybody adequate guidance from the outset, telling them what is expected on the job. Most of the time, unfortunately, no one is quite sure about what ought to be happening: the manager has one set of objectives in mind, the subordinate another. Each has a different SHOULD against which to assess ACTUAL performance. Under these conditions nobody can be completely satisfied with what gets done. One sees a deviation where the other has no inkling that a deviation exists. If both manager and subordinate understand the same set of objectives for a job, they have a basis for communicating about it, for evaluating performance, for discussing changes that need to be made, and for handling problems that arise. *Each person is proceeding from a known, visible, measured framework for behavior.*

Making the ground rules clear at the outset prevents a host of future problems. The more explicit the objectives, the better. Weights need to be assigned to the various dimensions, for all are not of the same significance. Although manager and subordinate may initially see the objectives in common, they may have widely differing views on how much emphasis each should receive. Job objectives are often separated into MUSTS and WANTS: the former are *mandatory* performance criteria, the latter *desirable* criteria.

Some of our clients speak of "emphasis areas"—that is, performance objectives that designate a specific percentage of the total effort. "Customer service, 40%," for instance, means that the employee is expected to devote nearly half of all energy toward this target. It also means that the employee should not go overboard, doing nothing but customer service. The degree of guidance a manager can give an employee depends on the explicitness and quantity of these objectives. Performance objectives are especially helpful for low performers. Such people often have the greatest difficulty in figuring out what the boss has in mind.

One major benefit of clear performance objectives is the hiring of fewer average performers. Once a 50% performer is on board and part of your organization, you are assured of a constant source of headaches and frustration. Easier said than done, of course. However, when you develop job performance objectives for use as selection criteria, you have taken a long step in the right direction. The more nearly the hired person fits the demands of the job, the more likely will be his or her success in the job. What do you really want this person to do? Equally important, what do you want the person *not* to do?

When a job calls for tact in dealing with peers and clients, recognize this requirement as an important characteristic. Don't hire an abrasive, insensitive person. If such a person is hired, the ultimate fault lies in the organization's failure to do its homework adequately.

Systematically Evaluating ALTERNATIVES

When our alternatives consist of people or of actions that affect people, our evaluation must be especially careful and systematic. How much more palatable it must be to a person to know that he or she has been assessed openly against stated objectives, than to have the feeling that the future has been decided by a mysterious lottery. People deserve the best treatment they can get, and honest evaluation of their efforts goes a long way toward meeting that need. When we manage human performance problems, the communicative advantages of a visible, systematic evaluation of alternatives are enormous. In any selection situation, someone wins and someone else loses. The fact that a *systematic* evaluation has been made brings credit to the organization.

The trick lies in getting pertinent data. Only then do we have a sound basis for making a judgment. Take, for example, hiring decisions. People being interviewed for jobs are on best behavior. They all are at their most atypical level. Their responses are slanted in what they judge to be the most acceptable manner. Their abrasiveness (if they normally are abrasive) is carefully controlled. Their insensitivity (if they normally are insensitive) never appears. Job candidates wish to sell themselves. Consciously or unconsciously, they will do all in their power to appear to be the answer to the organization's prayers. Seldom are personality cosmetics applied as generously as in the job interview.

Past performance can be the best source of valid information—provided that the right questions are asked. Prospective employers are unfortunately hesitant about asking straight, hard questions about a candidate. Past employers are understandably hesitant about giving specific information if they are not asked for it. However, they usually supply the facts if the right questions come up.

Assessing CONSEQUENCES Good and Bad

In human performance problems, assessing consequences is an attempt to protect an employee's future against unintended harm. For example, where travel constitutes an adverse consequence, a hardship, and an intolerable strain on a particular employee's family, it would be wrong for an organization to promote that employee to a position requiring a great deal of travel.

All factors must be taken into consideration. Actions affecting human beings have multiple consequences—some good, some harmful. Fairness requires at the least that any unintended effects be assessed. The organization should not decide for the employee how life in the future should be lived; rather, it must be aware of how today's decisions may affect tomorrow's conditions.

Consequences are not always adverse. Some of our clients have begun to provide day-care service for the children of employees so that mothers can work. The positive consequences of this action—increased employee commitment to the organization and reduced turnover—have been significant. The search for positive consequences—a so-called opportunity analysis—can be a source of added productivity and satisfaction for everyone concerned.

Preventing POTENTIAL PROBLEMS

The best kind of performance problem is one that we have anticipated and prevented: The employee is spared unnecessary harm, and the organization has avoided confusion and disruption. Everything continues as it should, and everyone's energies are focused on the job to be done.

Potential Problem Analysis is the prime tool of the manager of human performance. It is usually done implicitly, informally. When a manager must take an action that will affect someone in the organization, the manager reviews the potential problems: "I won't put those two together—the chemistry won't be right." "Stratton is relatively new to the job. He'll need more supervision than the others at first. I'd better assign Linda to keep an eye on him, help him out." This is the kind of thinking that pays big dividends. If ever the maxim "Look before you leap" makes sense, it is in the area of human performance problems. In all matters of human resource management, the best time to recognize trouble is *before* the fact—not when feelings have already been hurt, when people are angry and frustrated, and when productivity has fallen.

Performance Problems: Challenge and Response

The New Computer Operator

Often, in dealing with a performance problem, good management of the problem requires that the manager pinpoint the true cause of the deviation; adaptive action is simply not good enough. Such a case calls for use of the entire Problem Analysis process. In the following example, what begins as an apparently typical personnel problem ultimately produces an unexpected explanation. Note the inadequacy of any action that may be taken, as long as cause remains unknown.

> An insurance company was heavily involved in trusts and retirement funds. The investments section in its main office updated client accounts on a daily basis. Operators would query the computer record, read the desired information from the display console, enter the new information into the computer, and send the modified data back into memory. Although this critical function was protected by error-checking devices, operator accuracy was paramount. All transactions were handled on three display consoles, and the expected error rate was about 1%.

In April of one year, a number of changes were made in the investments section. The entire area was redecorated and made more pleasant for the operators. Dingy walls were repainted in bright, light colors, and new draperies were hung. Equipment was relocated in a more informal arrangement. Many employees commented favorably on the changes, and morale seemed to improve substantially. When one of the console operators was promoted, a young woman was moved from a computer position in another department to take the operator's place on the Number Two Console.

By mid-May it was apparent that the section had a problem with the new transfer. She was a loner. She ate lunch by herself, usually with a book as a companion, and was unwilling to join in office small talk. This irritated several of her coworkers. The young woman was pleasant enough, but never initiated a conversation. Besides, her attitude toward the job seemed questionable.

Yet she did an adequate job—until about the first of June. At that time her error rate climbed from the normal 1% to nearly 10%. Her supervisor had a talk with her, and the error rate dropped to normal for a couple of days. But then it climbed back to 10%. The supervisor talked with her again. This time the woman responded poorly, complaining sullenly about the work and about headaches. There was no improvement.

By the middle of June the situation had become intolerable. The woman was transferred to another department and a less demanding job. The operator of Number One Console was shifted to Number Two, and a new person, recently trained, was put on Number One. The error rate promptly dropped to normal.

Two days later the error rate on Number Two Console jumped to 10%—although it was now in the hands of a seasoned operator. The error rate remained stable at 1% on the other two consoles, one of which was operated by the new, recently trained employee. The situation made no sense at all to the supervisor.

A team was formed to look into the matter and find an explanation for the high error rate on the Number Two Console. A meticulous examination of the console was completed; nothing was wrong with the console. Then a comparative specification was drawn up. Number Two Console was compared with the other two consoles. Its operator was compared with the other two operators. Days of high error were identified and compared with days of good performance. The analysis produced no reasonable explanations for the sporadically high error rate.

The computer manufacturer sent in representatives to examine all the consoles, but they couldn't account for the trouble. The study team returned to its initial specification and asked, in each dimension of the specification, "What *could* explain this comparative information?" When they considered the dimension of *timing,* comparing days of high error with days of normal error, someone said, "How about sunspots? We've tried everything else!" Everyone laughed and then someone remarked: "Sunspots . . .sun. . .weather. . .what about *weather*?"

It was the season of spring and early summer showers. Some days were bright and sunny, few overcast and rainy. "So what? It rains every spring, and *this* is the spring we have the trouble!" But then they looked at the consoles. They saw that Number Two Console was located near a large window in the south wall of the building. And they noticed that the new draperies were of a light color and loose weave. *Sunlight!* Obviously, on bright days enough light could come in through those draperies to make it difficult to read the display. This could easily cause errors (and headaches). But on overcast days, with less outside light, the display would be clearer and easier to read accurately.

Weather statistics were checked out, and the cause was verified: overcast days were the 1%-error days.

The loner who had preferred to eat lunch by herself, who complained of headaches continued to hold the less demanding job. For various reasons the company felt it was "too embarrassing" to return the woman to her old job at Number Two Console.

This can only suggest that more thorough testing of cause should have been carried out *before* the adaptive action (transferring the woman) was taken. Even at that time there was enough information to show that cause lay in another direction. Management of human performance problems demands that we be as nearly right in our conclusions and actions as we can be. When mistakes are made, the losers are usually innocent bystanders.

Our Boy Genius

No one argues the point that there is great diversity among human beings. Yet, when we are investigating a human performance problem, we seldom focus on one aspect of this diversity: the effects of past work experiences on current performance. Even when this information is available, we may be too late in understanding its implications. This mistake is illustrated in the following example.

The space industry expands and contracts in response to the flow of appropriations from Congress. It was in a period of cutback that a highly touted young engineer was transferred from one organization to another. Despite his youth Roy came with a solid-gold record of achievement. His new boss considered the transfer a great coup.

But Roy just couldn't seem to settle down and get things done. When you put him on a project, before you knew it, he'd be off on some nutty tangent that had little or nothing to do with his assignment. He seemed totally undisciplined and continually overreached his authority. On top of everything, when his boss finally criticized him for his behavior, Roy was totally surprised—and then he got mad: "I don't get to make any decisions anymore!" His boss replied that that was preposterous—Roy had shown no decision-making ability at all since the day he joined the organization. Roy replied heatedly that he had been "knocking himself out" and "doing a great job." The meeting ended on a bitter note.

In the wake of Roy's stormy exit, the manager sat and wondered: What was really going on? Roy's youth? Excessive enthusiasm? Or was he simply a bright nut who'd had a couple of lucky breaks in his past job? The manager decided to try Problem Analysis techniques in order to get a better understanding of the Roy problem.

He carefully specified the situation in terms of Identity, Location, Timing, and Magnitude. In the dimension of Location, he wrote "IS. . .in this organization." He looked over at the space on the page under "Location: could be but IS NOT. . ." and then stopped short. He had always assumed that Roy's work in his previous job had gone fine. The recommendations certainly indicated that. He needed to get detailed, factual information on exactly what Roy *had* done before. Setting aside the analysis, he picked up the phone and began to do some research.

He talked to a number of people who had worked with Roy in the past. They all thought he was just great. The manager asked: What had Roy done? Why, he'd held a sort of roving assignment. He was the hotshot who did anything and everything, who probed into whatever interested and challenged him. How had he got away with that? Well, at the time, there had been so much work, so many potentially useful projects in sight, so many directions in need of exploration, that Roy's mode of operation was not only tolerated but welcomed. There were always plenty of workers available. . .Roy was what you might call a minor chief. Nicknamed "our boy genius" by his colleagues, whom he didn't see very often, he had been the individual contributor *par excellence*.

Would he be likely to do well in a more routine job? "Roy? Hell, no!" said one of his old friends. "He'd be like a meteoric square peg in a slow round hole. . . ."

Before the manager had time to resolve the problem, Roy decided to quit. He gave the reason that "this place doesn't suit me." (It didn't.) But the manager suspected that he might have salvaged an extremely bright engineer for his organization if he had not waited so long to start a systematic analysis of the problem.

This story illustrates two important elements common to many performance problems. The first is that *unacceptable behavior was the result of the positive effect such behavior had had in the past*. In his earlier job the man had been rewarded for doing exactly the thing that would get him into trouble in a job with very different requirements. No wonder that Roy was surprised and angry when his new boss criticized him for doing what he had always done and been praised for doing. Roy had been unaware that the rules of the game had changed.

Such a cause for unacceptable performance, especially in a new or transferred employee, is so common that it deserves serious consideration in a case of inexplicable behavior. Comparing past and present jobs may bring out the fact that previous rules and expectations, now made visible, are at the core of the problem. As long as such a fundamental misunderstanding exists between manager and subordinate, any attempt at communication will be endless and fruitless.

The second element common to problems with people is *inadvertent lack of attention to what is being said*. When we asked this manager, a year after the incident, "What did Roy himself *say* about his work situation?" he recounted the bitter conversation in his office. In his Problem Analysis the manager had carefully listed Roy's faults—unreliability, overreaching of authority, and so on—but he had not included anything Roy had actually *said*. Had he considered Roy's statements as behavior, he might well have followed up on the critical remark "I don't get to make decisions *anymore*" to learn exactly what Roy meant.

The sheer visibility of such a remark can help a manager consider its implications. Then he or she can decide how best to discuss the problem with the employee. The uncommunicative meeting between these two men (the manager missed the import of Roy's complaint) could hardly provide valuable insights into the nature of the problem, much less its cause. Had the manager used a complete specification of the problem (including words *and* deeds) as the basis for the second meeting, differences might have been resolved and a mutually acceptable PERFORMANCE SHOULD established.

It is not always easy to determine the relevancy of a particular remark. It is essential, however, that we make an effort to understand both its meaning and its source. There is something distasteful about including angry remarks or gripes as part of an analytical process. To many people, such information smacks of gossip. But if the gripe is part of the problem situation, rather than hearsay or secondhand information, then it ought to be included. Someone's remark may contain clues to the cause of the problem. We have to be alert to that possibility and we have to *listen*. A remark such as "I don't get to make decisions *anymore*" clearly deserves attention. It should have been considered as part of the problem's *identity,* along with all the other descriptive information on Roy's behavior.

"Nobody Can Stand Carl"

Almost anyone can manage great performers—people who always do more than is expected, who initiate ideas, who are blessed with impeccable judgment, who are well liked by everyone. It is the ability to get the best performance from the *average* person that is the mark of excellence.

> Carl was a bright young Ph.D., newly assigned to a staff position in a United States government agency. His competence and enthusiasm were unquestioned, he loved his work, and he worked harder than anyone on the staff. After six months on the job, his manager was about to fire him. Why? Because Carl could not get along with people. Carl had approached the agency with a superb resume; during his interviews he had impressed everyone. In fact when Carl first agreed to come to work for him, the manager had been absolutely delighted.
>
> But things had not worked out delightfully. Carl was arrogant with subordinates, abrasive with peers, and rude to the agency's clients. Every meeting he attended turned into a shouting match. His behavior had become a grim joke throughout the agency, but his boss wasn't laughing. "I finally checked back with the guy he used to report to, and he said Carl had always been that way. 'Sure, he *produced,* but nobody could *stand* him.' And he had written such a glowing letter about Carl. . .well, that's typical. People just don't like to write negatives in those letters, do they?"
>
> The manager wanted to find the least painful way to get rid of Carl. As a first step he specified Carl's performance, listing all unacceptable features in the IS column, and all good features in the IS NOT column. He was using a fragment of the Problem Analysis process to make the nature of Carl's performance visible. In this way he could see how to deal with it. It was not a cause-finding effort; the problem's cause was perfectly apparent. The more the manager wrote, the more he thought through the situation, the more he became convinced that Carl—whatever his shortcomings of personality—was a valuable employee who should not be fired or transferred!
>
> The information under "IS NOT a problem" consumed far more space than did the information on the other side. For all his faults Carl was reliable, punctual, flexible, and willing to take on unpopular assignments. He showed great originality of thought and unflagging initiative. As a matter of fact, not only did Carl shine in these areas, he outshone most of his peers.

The manager realized that he had lost his sense of proportion in his obsession with Carl's personality flaws. If he fired Carl he would lose much-needed skills, with no adequate replacement in sight. For a week or two the rest of the staff would be grateful . . .and then? The manager estimated that within two months the department would be unable to keep up with its workload, and would have far worse problems than those caused by Carl's bad temper and insensitivity. The chances of quickly finding a new employee with Carl's training and ability were virtually nil.

The manager then began a tentative restructuring of Carl's job. It would severely limit Carl's contacts with agency staff and with client representatives while actually increasing Carl's level of autonomy and responsibility. How did he achieve that? Origination of proposals within the department was currently split among five staff members, each one spending about 10% of his or her time in this function. Henceforth, the majority of such work would be Carl's. The manager found that plan acceptable to nearly everyone. Besides, Carl preferred that kind of work, viewing it as more creative than the endless paperwork that was second nature to other people on the staff. Carl was also given a variety of responsibilities for other work that was unpopular with his peers but acceptable to Carl. While this was neither a perfect solution nor a perfect plan, the manager now had a workable course of action.

Two months later the manager reassessed the actions he had taken. The job restructuring, he said, had been successful "to a degree of about six on a scale of one-to-ten." Although he was quietly on the lookout for a possible replacement for Carl, the manager emphasized that firing Carl in a moment of anger and frustration would have been a terrible mistake.

We are seldom able to turn the Carls of this world into likable people. As managers we have to work with and through all kinds of people, some disliked by their peers, some by us. But people with unpleasant personalities may possess valuable skills. To use these skilled people properly, we must assess them rationally and dispassionately. By specifying "IS a problem" from "IS NOT a problem" characteristics, we can take a great step toward seeing everything in correct proportion.

Honesty in Dealing with People

How better to conclude this chapter than to say that one should be fair and decent in dealing with people? And how better to *behave in that manner* than by making full and objective use of the information available, whether it be for Problem Analysis, Decision Analysis, or Potential Problem Analysis?

Few things hurt productivity more than having people think they have been dealt with unfairly, arbitrarily, or without the intention of understanding their views and positions. Asked with skill and courtesy, the kinds of questions we use in Problem Analysis, Decision Analysis, and Potential Problem Analysis cannot help but improve matters for everyone concerned.

One of the best examples of such use was supplied to us by Mr. R. B. Seidel, President of Automatic Timing and Controls Company, for use in the *Kepner-Tregoe Journal*. It represents the *management of human performance problems* in an almost ideal way. The following is quoted from his letter of January 16, 1978:

> I am including the Qualification & Capability Objectives for ATC Controller that were discussed in the recent [*Journal*] article to which you refer. . . . The list of Objectives, Musts, and Wants, along with the weighting, was developed by the key people in the Financial Department, who in fact would be working for the new Controller, along with some input and massaging from the Top Management Committee, who would be the peers of the new Controller. Therefore, everyone who had a stake in the outcome had a voice in the input of criteria.

> We gave the list of objectives to the candidates when they came in and they spent the entire first day with the key people in the Finance Department who would be working for them, asking questions and finding out how our system worked. Ostensibly they were gathering information to enable them to make a more or less prepared presentation to our entire Management Committee of their qualifications against our objectives and in light of the job as they understand it. Actually, at the end of the first day, I held a meeting with all of the key people in the Finance Department who had spent time with them, and there followed a free and open discussion evaluating their experience. Although I had not promised them the right to blackball any candidate, at least sixty percent of the candidates did not get invited back for good and sufficient reasons that came out of those discussions. All of the candidates that did get invited back had the willing approval of the people who would be working for them. I considered this to be a very valuable attribute of this method since to a large measure a man's ability to be successful in an organization is dependent on the willingness of people working for him to accept his leadership.

> [Each candidate] who was invited back was asked to make a presentation to the assembled Management Committee, with whom he would be working as a colleague. This presentation was to give all of the educational, work experience, and other back-

ground that would enable us to evaluate and score him on the particular objective in point.

It all worked out very well, and, in my opinion, the most important element was that of involving the people who would be working for him so intimately in the selection process.

Chapter Summary

To manage or solve people problems? It doesn't really make much difference. The important thing is to treat people fairly and honestly, making full use of all relevant information. This means knowing and communicating the objectives of a job so that everyone understands the rules of the game in the same way. It means asking for, getting, and using accurate data on which to base decisions. A large share of human performance problems are handled by managers who control and change the environment surrounding the job to help people adapt to the requirements of the job.

Managing human performance problems calls for a compassionate, considerate approach. Potential Problem Analysis, used as a thinking tool to identify and avoid future problems, is of the greatest importance. Bits and pieces of all thinking processes can be used as the situation warrants, to give people the benefit of every doubt. In this way the rational use of information does indeed achieve a better use of people as the organization's prime resource.

CHAPTER 9

Installing Rational Process Within an Organization

Introduction:
Ensuring That the Process Works

The examples of Rational Process used in the preceding chapters are representative, not unique. More than three thousand clients have similar examples in their files. Of course some have more and better examples than others. Since writing *The Rational Manager* in 1965, we have learned a great deal about the conditions under which Rational Process takes hold within an organization, keeps its momentum, and continues to pay off year after year. Through thousands of discussions with managers, we have learned what they *do* to achieve success with the ideas. And we have observed what organizations do—a month and a year and five years after the initial decision to install Rational Process ideas—to keep Rational Process alive and working.

There is nothing mysterious about the seven conditions for success with Rational Process that are described in this last chapter. Nor can there be much controversy about them. Clients who provide all seven conditions report invariably that they gain substantial, lasting benefits. Those who seriously neglect one or more find that use of the ideas dwindles away. The results that were initially projected or hoped for never materialize fully, or the ideas are used once in a while by a few enthusiasts. No organization wants that to happen, but it is the most likely consequence of the failure to provide one or more of the conditions that follow.

Seven Basic Conditions for Success

1.   *The results to be obtained and the objectives to be achieved through use of Rational Process ideas have been clearly defined and are understood and accepted by top management and participants alike. All personnel are committed to their use within the organization—at all levels and in all kinds of management situations.*

The installation of Rational Process is likely to succeed when people know what it is they are expected to learn, know how these ideas are to be used, believe that the ideas are useful, and are committed to putting them to work on behalf of the organization. Success is ensured when people know that top management understands, accepts, and uses the ideas and is fully committed to their application throughout the organization. Subordinates watch their superiors. They know that what superiors *do* can be more important than what superiors *say*. The validity of Rational Process is confirmed when top management shows by its own use of the ideas that the ideas work, and that they have been accepted as part of the organization's way of life.

2.   *The Rational Process ideas are presented in such a way that they are, first, immediately recognized as practical and beneficial to those who will use them; secondly, relevant to their specific jobs; and, finally, easy to transfer to the real, everyday situations with which they must deal.*

People do not resist practical and useful ideas that promise to be supportive of their own best interests. People do resist obscure theorizing that has no apparent helpful reference to their lives, threatens them because of its strangeness, and must be taken solely on faith. They accept the idea that prompts the immediate reaction "I can *use* that," especially if the second reaction is that personal payoff will follow. People use ideas that make sense and can be applied to their own areas of responsibility. The kind and quality of teaching through which the ideas are imparted are critical to the participants' success in their later use of the ideas in their real world.

3. *The application of Rational Process ideas to real concerns is not left to chance, but is guided and guaranteed through techniques that incorporate real problems and choices as teaching vehicles. In this way the first uses of the ideas occur as part of the process of learning them, ensuring success in their use as practical tools.*

People who learn something in a classroom or from a book are always faced with the question "But will it work for me when I really need it?" No matter how great the idea or technique may seem to be, it remains only theoretically great until it is used and found workable. Time may have elapsed and conditions become difficult and different. The ideas that once seemed so clear may be hard to recall and harder to put into practice. That is why the ideas of Rational Process are learned through demonstration. Relevance—to the needs of the individual and of the organization—is built in from the beginning.

4. *Systems and procedures within the organization are modified and redesigned to fit with, and capitalize on, the Rational Process ideas, thus institutionalizing their use. The four patterns of thinking become standard ways of operating.*

When ideas people have learned are unrelated to the way things are done in the organization, people must struggle to find opportunities to use their new knowledge. If the organization acts as a deterrent, a barrier to change, the struggle will be short-lived. When the systems and procedures of the organization have been modified to accommodate the use of new ideas, opportunities abound. The individual is pulled forward into new experiences, not restrained by the status quo.

5. *Rewards and personal satisfaction are provided to those who use Rational Process ideas to deal with the organization's concerns and decisions, and to those who supervise and manage the use of those ideas. Rational Process thus becomes first the preferred, eventually the automatic, way of thinking and working.*

People do those things that produce good results for them. When the use of Rational Process is rewarded by the organization, its use will be greater than it would be if there were no reward, no notice taken. When those who manage the use of Rational Process by others are rewarded for doing so, they will plan more uses for the future. Success in using the ideas perpetuates success only where specific, successful applications are made visible and are rewarded.

6. *There is continued follow-on activity to reinforce and sharpen capabilities already acquired, to extend application to new areas of organizational concern, and to reaffirm top management's commitment to the use of Rational Process.*

No attempt at change and improvement that is introduced as a one-shot effort, or that is perceived as such by the people expected to do the changing and improving, can be expected to have any lasting positive effects. The Rational Process ideas represent basic patterns of thinking, not "the latest approach" to problem solving or decision making. Yet use of the techniques derived from these basic patterns depends on follow-up and follow-on activities. A carefully planned program of extension and augmentation ensures that use of the ideas and their effectiveness will grow with time.

7. *There is continued monitoring and evaluation of the results of use of Rational Process, assessing progress against initial objectives, and providing feedback about these results to all concerned.*

Evaluation of results is vital. Beyond demonstrating to management what return is being realized from the investment of resources that has been made, evaluation of results provides the basis for further decisions about the use of Rational Process. Feedback of success information motivates users, since everyone likes to be on a winning team. A special application of the ideas developed in one sector of an organization, properly communicated, may be equally useful in another sector. Making such results visible throughout the organization does much to enhance success.

The Meaning of "Install"

We say that we *install* the ideas of Rational Process. This word has a special meaning for our clients and for us. Acquisition of Rational Process skills is not unlike acquisition of a major piece of capital equipment. Once it is acquired, you can expect it to work and produce as predicted only if it is properly installed and integrated into the functioning of the rest of the organization.

Rational Process is a set of tools for getting things done, for handling information productively so that problems are solved and successful decisions made. It can and should pay for itself many times over through increased productivity and money saved. Its results can and should be tangible, measurable, visible, and verifiable. Yet, as with most other things of value, what the user gets out of Rational Process is a function of what the organization puts into it, both at the outset and as the months and years go by.

What is implied in installation of Rational Process goes far beyond what we ordinarily understand as training. Training comprises bringing together a number of people, presenting them with a set of material to be learned, then releasing them back into the environment from which they came. Training is too often superficial and short-term in its results. It does some good but rarely leads to positive, permanent changes within the organization.

Successful installation of Rational Process comes about through careful planning and preparation. The objectives to be accomplished are *identified and actively embraced by top management*. The population of significant people—those who ultimately will use the ideas—is designated, and the sequence and schedule of exposure to the ideas are determined. Internal instructors—those who will teach the ideas to this significant population—are selected and prepared. Systems and procedures are redesigned to support continuing use of the ideas on everyday tasks and assignments. Follow-on activities are selected and scheduled. Reward systems are put in place and measurement procedures are developed. These are actions that ensure success.

As surely as a piece of complex capital equipment is installed within a plant system, Rational Process is installed within the system of relationships, roles, and responsibilities that make an organization what it is. Installation, in these terms, constitutes the framework within which the seven conditions for success can be provided.

Two Methods of Installing Rational Process

There are two distinct methods of installing Rational Process. A client organization may choose to follow one or the other, depending on which is more convenient and more compatible with the way the organization customarily operates. The first is the *Organizational Focus* method, in which Rational Process is introduced initially to deal with *specific organizational concerns*. With this method the ideas are seen as a top-management organizational tool for achieving preselected results.

The other is the *Individual Focus* method. A significant number of users are equipped to work with Rational Process ideas and then are directed toward targets of opportunity—that is, *concerns that lie within their areas of responsibility*.

Organizational Focus

The Organizational Focus method begins when someone at the very top level of management identifies a set of concerns that require analysis and correction. These concerns are of significant importance to the organization, rather than passing operational concerns. They are persistent, undesirable situations that have grown over time and have never been adequately addressed. It is clear that a major effort is required to solve them, and that new skills and approaches have to be developed if the effort is to be successful.

The entire project is planned as a task-force attack on situations identified *before* introduction of the ideas of Rational Process within the organization. Objectives are defined. These are: analysis and correction of the target situations, and the simultaneous installation of Rational Process as a working way of life within the organization. This planning cannot be delegated. It is done by top management, since responsibility for the project must reside with those who initiate it. By actively directing the project, top management makes its support of the ideas evident to everyone. By participating in the project throughout its life, top management retains control and ensures success.

In meetings with Kepner-Tregoe representatives, management works out a comprehensive plan and schedule. The population of individuals who can contribute to solving the target situations is identified by name and position. Workshops are scheduled. It is in the workshops that the participants will learn to use Rational Process. Later, they will apply their skills to analysis of their assigned concerns. Top management is included in this population. *All* who can contribute share in the learning experience. Teams of individuals who will work together on particular concerns attend workshops together.

Line managers are selected as internal instructors for the workshops. They are taught by Kepner-Tregoe to introduce and install the ideas and to act as Process Consultants, or resident experts, for the organization. Work is assigned to the participants. This consists of research into the backgrounds of designated organizational concerns, enabling the participants to bring current data to the workshop sessions. Then the workshops are held in rapid succession, preparing a critical mass of participants for effective action. As results are obtained and documented, this information is fed back to top management to guide further direction of the project and serve as a basis for evaluation.

Systems and procedures are redesigned concurrently to support and take advantage of Rational Process. Meetings, repetitive activities, and organizational communications are streamlined to fit in with the ideas. Informal reward systems of recognition and appreciation are set up to motivate participants who have made good use of the ideas. Formal rewards are instituted for outstanding achievers. Follow-on activities are established to sharpen and extend skills.

As the project moves forward and selected organizational problems are solved and corrected, the ideas of Rational Process become institutionalized within the organization. These ideas become standard ways of operating. For the individuals involved, the ideas become internalized and second nature. People share a common language and a common orientation toward problems, choices, and concerns about the future. Other populations then are drawn in, exposed to the ideas, and assigned new problem situations for analysis and correction. Eventually, everyone who can productively use Rational Process is exposed to its ideas.

With the expansion of the population of individuals using the ideas, more daily operational problems are attacked. New targets of opportunity are addressed. Use of the ideas becomes a fundamental part of the way the organization conducts its business at all levels. The measurement of results continues, as does feedback to management and participants. It is important that everyone understand what has been accomplished. In any organization that installs Rational Process, there is no day on which the effort is complete, no end to the program.

Individual Focus

The Individual Focus method of installing Rational Process begins when someone at an upper level of management realizes that there is a need for improvement of problem-analysis and decision-analysis skills in the organization. The focus is on the individual users—people whose skills are to be upgraded through introduction of Rational Process. It is accepted that if those involved in significant matters in the organization deal with those matters in a more efficient and thorough manner, the productivity of the entire organization will increase.

The project is conceived as a program of human resource development. The objectives to be set have to do with improving the capabilities of significant personnel. Plans for putting such a program into effect are usually, but not always, delegated to an appropriate staff function. Top management may participate in the program, often to the extent of attending an abbreviated version of the Rational Process Workshop. But this participation does not entail the deep personal involvement of top management that characterizes the organizationally-focused program. Commitment to the usefulness of the ideas may be just as great, but the resolve to use the ideas personally on a day-to-day basis may fall short.

In meetings with Kepner-Tregoe representatives, those assigned by their organization to plan and organize the program work out a schedule of events. Individuals to be included are identified by name and position. Workshops are scheduled. Functional, or *family*, groups—people who customarily work together or share information—are formed as workshop teams. Line managers are selected as internal instructors for the workshops and are taught by Kepner-Tregoe to introduce and install the ideas and to act as Process Consultants.

To this extent the individually-focused program is identical with the organizationally-focused program. A major difference between them is the nature of the work that participants are required to do before attending a workshop. In the individually-focused program, each participant researches and brings in problems and choice situations *from his or her own job*. The participant's superior may become involved in the selection of these situations. An important problem or decision that requires the inputs of several people may suggest that these people should attend the same workshop. In this way it is possible to mount task forces to deal with specific situations within an individually-focused program.

The workshops are then held according to schedule. The participants apply their new skills to their own problem situations, continue to work on them back on the job, and sometimes share their skills with coworkers. Initiative to use the ideas generally comes from the individual user, who is encouraged by the workshop leader acting as Process Consultant to push individual or team applications to successful completion. As results are obtained and documented, they are fed back to superiors and to top management. These results assist management in evaluating the program's impact, and in revising or expanding its direction and purpose.

Systems and procedures may be redesigned to support and take advantage of Rational Process. In the individually-focused program, these steps are usually taken in response to individual user demand. They cannot be taken at all, however, until enough people have been exposed to Rational Process to make the steps worthwhile. Since formation of a critical mass of people able to use and share the ideas is not a keystone of the individually-focused program, revision of systems and procedures to fit with Rational Process methods often takes place on an ad hoc basis.

Informal and formal reward systems are set up as additional motivation for those who have made good use of the ideas. Such systems usually have lower visibility than they do in the organizationally-focused program. Like the original workshops, follow-on activities reflect the specific needs of individual users.

As more and more people within the organization become users, the ideas of Rational Process gradually become institutionalized as the preferred way of operating. Users internalize the ideas and draw on them as needed. They also share the ideas of Rational Process with others who have been exposed to them. In the individually-focused approach, Rational Process tends to be "catching". In one very common situation, we find six people assigned to formulation of a decision. Four of them are able to use Decision Analysis, and the other two will be assigned to a Rational Process Workshop. In this way the entire team can use a common approach in arriving at decisions.

Application of the ideas spreads to all levels of the organization until the use of Rational Process occurs routinely in daily situations. At this point people will be bringing the ideas to bear on organizational concerns faced both by units and the corporation as a whole. Feedback to management and individual users continues. The measurement of results continues.

A Comparison and a Recommendation

Neither Organizational Focus nor Individual Focus is inherently superior. Those of our clients who have achieved substantial increases in productivity through use of Rational Process are found in each camp in about equal numbers. Success lies not in how the ideas are introduced but in the degree to which the seven essential conditions are provided to support and perpetuate Rational Process within the organization.

Organizational Focus requires a greater commitment of time and effort on the part of top management as well as active participation in the project from the start. That participation must be maintained indefinitely. It implies a higher degree of urgency. It aims at achievement of specific organizational results at the outset, rather than later on, as the program matures. It provides top management with more control over the investment. Introduction of the ideas of Rational Process usually is rapid and pervasive, because it is important to build a critical mass of users as soon as possible.

Individual Focus, on the other hand, places more reliance on such staff functions as human resource planning or personnel development. It places more reliance on the individual user to find opportunities for application and to carry these forward to successful conclusion. It provides unit managers, rather than top management, with the desired degree of control over use of Rational Process. Individual Focus is usually a long-term, continuing effort conducted on many fronts.

The choice of method must be made by the individual client organization. Which fits better? Which accomplishes better the objectives of the organization? Which is more compatible with the way the organization chooses to operate? As long as the seven conditions for success are understood and provided, either method produces tangible, substantial benefits for the organization.

Nevertheless, all things being equal, when we are asked to recommend one approach over the other, we recommend Organizational Focus. Our experience has shown that *active involvement of top management* in planning and executing any activity gives that effort a higher probability of success. So it is when installing Rational Process. When top management adopts a new way of doing things, people take note and guide their actions accordingly.

Management involvement, however, is a two-edged sword. If top management appears insincere about the commitment, everyone will perceive that lack of wholehearted interest. Presuming that the Organizational Focus is wholeheartedly embraced and that the seven conditions are met, the expectation for a successful program is excellent. Greater benefits will be experienced through Organizational Focus in a shorter period of time than will be experienced through Individual Focus.

There are hybrid approaches that lie somewhere between the two methods. Some of our clients have begun with an Individual Focus and then moved to an Organizational Focus as top management became involved. In some cases middle managers were exposed to Rational Process ten or fifteen years ago, within an individually-focused program. Now they are top management, and they control and maintain a Rational Process program that is clearly focused on organizational problems and concerns.

One thing is clear. If an individually-focused program never moves to the point at which significant organizational concerns are approached and resolved through Rational Process ideas, the organization's investment has paid off only a fraction of its potential. Upgrading of management skills is a worthwhile objective, but we are eager to see organizations realize every possible benefit from their relationship with us. We are equally concerned with upgrading Rational Process programs that have lagged or that have failed to produce results as rapidly and dramatically as expected. Our business is only tangentially concerned with *programs*. It is centered on producing *results*.

Rational Management

The goal of Rational Management is to make full use of the thinking ability of the people of the organization and to direct that ability toward meeting the organization's problems and concerns.

This goal is achieved by giving people the conceptual tools they need to do the job, a set of methods and techniques they can share as they gather and handle information to resolve problems, make choices, anticipate future concerns, and break complex situations into manageable components. In addition the organization must provide its people with a supportive framework within which coordinated use of these ideas by the team can flourish.

Rational Management cannot just happen. Rational Management must be planned and managed into being as a planned intervention. It represents a major change in the way the organization operates, so it must be introduced by top management. If Rational Management is to succeed fully, a major commitment must be made, and particular conditions must be met.

The four patterns of thinking most widely used in the day-to-day work of an organization—finding cause, choosing the best course of action, foreseeing future problems, and rendering a complex situation manageable—can be sharpened and made more productive through installation of Rational Process. When this is carefully done, the productivity of the entire organization increases. Responsibility for quality moves in ever-widening circles from the organization's center. More people contribute in a significant way, because they learn how to coordinate their thinking with the thinking of others for the good of all.

Rational Management presides over no miracles. It releases intellectual resources that have been hidden, unused, or underused. It opens channels of communication among people by giving them common approaches and a common language for dealing with the ordinary and extraordinary situations they face in their jobs. Installation of Rational Process ideas makes it possible for the organization to be more nearly what every manager always believed it could be but too seldom was: an effective, efficient, and dynamic entity.

INDEX